magickal KNICKERS

and other ways to create a life of intention

RECLAIM THE MAGICK OF YOU

- - - - - - - - - - - - - -

Design by GW Illustration
www.GrantWickham.co.uk

 RebeccaAnuwen.com

 facebook.com/themodernwitchway

 instagram.com/themodernwitchway

Dedication

To my incredible husband Jamie, our magickal son Solomon, and our adventurous Weimaraner puppy Merlin: my living proof of what's possible when you embody your magick.

Magickal Bonuses!

Visit: https://rebeccaanuwen.com/magickalbonuses
or open the camera on your phone and scan the QR code
to access your bonus content.

BONUS #1

MAGICKAL KNICKERS: INSTRUCTION MANUAL (PDF)

Use the Magickal Knickers: Instruction Manual PDF to explore
the exercises in the book and uncover the magick of you

BONUS #2

THE MAGICKAL KNICKER DRAWER (EXCLUSIVE PODCAST)

Be guided through rituals and activities from the book,
with additional suggestions on how you can incorporate
them, or something similar, to your day.

With love and bonus magick

Rebecca
xx

Table of Contents

Introduction

Once upon a time...

Once upon a time, you were utterly unafraid to be who you were.

For the first few years of your life, you listened to your body, honoured your needs and followed your heart. You sang loudly, danced wildly and dressed to please only yourself.

You knew exactly what you wanted from each moment, and you were deeply, inextricably connected to your power and your magick. But over time, the thoughts, opinions and expectations of friends, family and society in general eroded that connection.

It probably didn't happen all at once. Instead, as erosion does, it took time. It happened in a slow, steady drip, drip, drip – one drip every time you realised you couldn't stay true to yourself and still:

- please everyone you cared about

- keep being 'the good girl'

- know for sure that the people around you would love the real you

- fit in and feel a sense of belonging and community

- avoid the risk of making a fuss or coming across as bossy or selfish

------ / ------

Then, those drips grew larger and heavier once you began getting positive reinforcement for being less you. You probably got complimented and praised every time you:

- put someone else's needs before your own

- sacrificed time you'd planned to spend doing an activity you enjoyed for an event that was important to someone else

- deferred to someone else, even when you knew you were right, just to keep the peace

And with each 'drip' that eroded your belief in yourself and what YOU wanted from your life, you also weakened your connection to your magick. (We'll talk about why in *Section 2: Your Magickal Life Philosophy*.)

How much in your life are you putting off?

We all know that our time on Earth is limited. And yet, this isn't the story we tell ourselves.

Instead, we say, "I'll do it later. I'll follow my desire when the time is right."

We say,

- "I'll finally learn that style of cooking when..."

- "I'll travel to the places I've always longed to see when..."

- "I'll read that book, schedule that massage or start getting fitter when..."

And then comes the 'when': "I'll do it when...

- ... I have more time."

- ... the kids have left home."

- ... the people around me don't need me as much."

- ... I feel more confident."

- ... I have the right qualification or experience."

When that thing – whatever it is – finally happens, THEN we can live how we want to live.

THEN we can do all that we've planned and dreamed of.

Later may be too late

We're here in our human bodies for a very limited amount of time. In his book *Four Thousand Weeks*, British Journalist Oliver Burkeman notes that the average life is 'insultingly, absurdly brief'.

If we live to be 80, he says, that works out as just a little under the 4,000 weeks from the book's title.

It's a sobering thought, isn't it? Put that way, it really doesn't sound like much time.

Certainly, at the age of seven, my little boy didn't think so when he heard his dad and me talking about this being an average lifespan.

Granted, his perception of time wasn't the most accurate at that age. He was sure that a four-hour trip to see family actually took 'a hundred hours'.

Still though, he's not wrong about 4,000 weeks being a short time – especially when so many of us live our lives as though we'll have forever.

We forget that life is finite. We put the things we most want on hold until some future condition is met. We just assume that we'll always have tomorrow.

But living this way means the present never feels fulfilling. There's always *something* else to do or someone else who wants our attention.

It's time to prioritise yourself

When I was a child, we'd often go to my Nan's house for dinner. I remember her telling us to eat our favourite part of the meal first. If we left it to the end, she said, we might not have room for it.

This went directly against what my mum had always told us. "Eat your vegetables first," she used to say. "They're good for you!"

One night, Nan made toad-in-the-hole – a classic British dish of sausages in batter. The sausages were my favourite part, but I dutifully ate all of my vegetables first. And of course, Nan was right. By the time I got to the sausages, I was far too full to enjoy eating them.

In the same vein, if you put the things you truly want off, you may never get to do them.

The truth is that you'll never check off *everything* on your to-do list. You'll never be completely free of responsibilities or other people's needs and expectations. The reward for a job well done is always more work. So the more organised and productive you become, the more you'll discover that needs doing.

And given that you're probably a significant way into your 4,000 weeks already, isn't it about time you started focusing on the things you want? On the *life* you want?

The secret is being more YOU

The fundamental concept behind *Magickal Knickers and other ways to create a life of intention* is helping you to 'be more you'.

It's not a book about goal-setting, at least not in the traditional sense. I'm not going to give you a precise, step-by-step action plan to help you set a specific goal and then see it through to fruition.

This isn't a grimoire (a recipe book of spells that you can cast to achieve different desires) either. Although, to be fair, you could frame many of the activities I offer throughout the book as 'spells' if that's the way you'd like to see them. You don't have to, but it's absolutely an option.

Nor is this a book about manifesting – or again, not in the way that most people teach it.

Granted, I do use the word 'manifesting' to mean 'bringing into reality' from time to time. But I'm not going to tell you to pick a desire and then just sit back and visualise it coming to you while you focus on nothing more than maintaining good vibes. Nor will I insist that if you don't already have what you want, it's because you let that single negative thought creep in yesterday.

Instead, I'm going to explain how identifying and then achieving what you want from life comes down to simply 'being more you'.

It starts with recognising the value of your dreams and desires, your ideas, your sense of humour and your quirks – all the things that make you uniquely 'you' – and the home of all of this: your body.

It also involves accepting, embracing and celebrating all that you truly are. It involves embodying the full spectrum of 'you' in all your highs and lows:

- the fully expressed parts and the work-in-progress parts

- the put-together parts and the wild, uncomfortable parts

- the quiet parts and the so-called 'too much' parts (*especially* those 'too much' parts!)

Being more you is also about giving yourself permission to follow your curiosity – to change your mind and then change it again. It's about doing more of what lights you up and makes you feel more like you, regardless of what those around you do, say or think.

It's also about refusing to wait to be 'perfect', or more healed, or more educated, or happier before you start moving towards your dreams and desires. It's about knowing that you can take action and create change, from wherever you are in your life right now, no matter how that looks or feels.

Finally, it's about unapologetically claiming your power, believing in yourself and having your own back. This involves fuelling yourself with your internal desires, rather than looking for external validation.

That's exactly *why* I'm not going to give you a precise, step-by-step action plan, by the way. You and I are very different people. What works for me won't necessarily work for you. It might not even keep working for me as I grow and evolve and change over time. So how could I possibly tell you exactly what you should do or how you should do it?

Instead, I want this book to provide a general roadmap to help you connect with and tap into your own inner wisdom and power. I want it to show you how to use your inner knowing to identify your desires and then bring them into being.

And I want it to do all that through a buffet of options and activities you can pick and choose between. As you experiment, I want you to always know you have total freedom to modify (or completely ignore) anything that doesn't work for you as I've written it.

So what's the deal with magickal knickers?

Right now, if you've never worked with me before, you might be saying, "That's all very well, Rebecca. But what do magickal knickers have to do with being more of who I am? Do I have to cast some kind of spell on my underwear to reconnect with my magick?"

Well, no... it's more about the fact that little things matter.

There's magick in all kinds of small, everyday, mundane objects. Everything you surround yourself with can affect you in ways that are sometimes too subtle to notice unless you're paying close attention. Everything you watch, listen to, read, eat, drink, smell, touch or – yes – wear can make you feel a certain way and change your energy.

Maybe the scent of lavender makes you think of the grandmother you loved spending time with as a child. So whenever you smell it as an adult, you instantly feel safer and more peaceful.

Maybe bright red lipstick makes you feel confident enough to take on the world.

Maybe the soft, smooth glide of the perfect pen over the perfect planner paper makes you feel like someone who finally has their life together (or maybe that's just me?)

Regardless, part of reconnecting with the Magick of You is identifying what you can surround yourself with that will help you to be more of who you truly are. Perhaps you need to access more courage to step away from an expectation you've always felt trapped by, so you can walk your own path. Or maybe you need to tap into a well of patience or self-compassion after something you tried didn't work out.

Whatever it may be, what can you use to access those qualities?

Knickers are just one of the many items you can choose to help you connect with whatever you need to access to 'be more you'. But there's something about putting on the perfect pair of knickers, which most people will never see, that can do wonders for the way you see yourself.

I've been aware of this ever since I was a child who desperately wanted a set of knickers with the days of the week on them. Later, when I got my very first paycheque from my very first job, I celebrated by buying myself the most beautiful and expensive lingerie I'd ever worn. Wearing it always made me feel like a million dollars.

I don't think I'm the only one who has this association with knickers, either.

A few years back now, I created an entire magickal activity around consciously choosing your underwear to set your energy for the day. (It's in *Chapter 2.4 – Using your Magickal Life Philosophy* if you're curious.) To this day, that activity remains a favourite with my community.

Besides, the whole idea of magickal knickers always makes me smile. It reminds me not to take myself, or my life, too seriously.

And now, more than ever, that feels like a valuable reminder.

How to use this book

To get the most out of this book and truly reconnect with the Magick of You, you're going to need to do more than just read it.

It's a bit like deciding to go to the gym because you want to get stronger or move more comfortably. You can read all the books you like on good workout form, and learn which moves help which muscles and which stretches free up which joints. But until you actually show up at the gym, stow your gear in a locker and get moving out on the gym floor, you're not going to see any progress.

However... just like when you go to the gym, it helps to know at least a bit about what you're going to do before you start doing it. Contrary to what many motivational speakers will tell you, simply taking action for the sake of taking action won't necessarily move you closer to your goal. That's like getting into your car and driving in a random direction, hoping that because you're no longer 'here', you'll magickally be 'there' instead (wherever 'there' might be for you).

So my recommendation is to read right through the book once from start to finish. This will give you a general feel for the concepts and practices I cover. It'll also help you get a sense of how those concepts all relate to each other, and which practices might be good places to start with your action-taking.

Plus, as you're reading, you might want to keep an eye out for any ideas that pop up about adapting the activities to suit your needs and lifestyle.

Then once you're ready, I'd suggest going back through the sections to identify exactly where you're going to start taking action. I've divided the book into five sections that move from general concepts through to specific individual actions and practices:

- **Section 1: Key Concepts** – these are the essential background concepts that underlie everything else in the book. They're topics like what exactly I mean when I use the term 'magick', the role of intuition, and how managing your energy and energetic hygiene can help you manifest your desires.

- **Section 2: Your Magickal Life Philosophy** – your life philosophy is your overall approach to life and your fundamental understanding of how the world works. It can either support or undermine your ability to 'be more you' and create the outcomes you most want in your life. In this section, we'll discuss how to create a supportive philosophy.

- **Section 3: Your Magickal Mindset** – while your philosophy is your long-term, overarching approach to life, your mindset is more of a temporary way of being. That doesn't make it any less powerful, though. In this section, we'll talk about why making your mindset more supportive isn't as simple as just deciding to think more positively. I'll also share some powerful techniques that have helped me, and many of my community members, to change our mindsets.

- **Section 4: Magickal Habits** – while a magickal mindset can definitely support you in taking action towards your dreams and desires, it won't do the work for you. So in this section, we'll explore how taking action often means building and maintaining helpful habits, and how to make those habits magickal.

- **Section 5: Magickal practices** – finally, in the last section, we'll look at how you can transform simple, everyday habits into sacred, powerful rituals and practices. I'll introduce you to two of my favourite rituals, and give you a wealth of options to customise them and make them work uniquely for you.

------ // ------

Many people will find that it makes the most sense to start at the beginning again and work through the book section by section. This will help them to create a general foundation of philosophy and mindset before they move into building specific habits and then creating rituals with those habits.

This might be perfect for you. Or, you might be in a place where you already HAVE a strong, supportive Magickal Life Philosophy. Maybe you've also done a vast amount of work on your mindset and now you're looking for specific ways to weave magickal habits or rituals into your everyday life.

If that's the case, feel free to ignore Sections 1 through 3 on your second readthrough, and jump straight to Section 4.

Once again, this book is about 'being more you'. It's about creating a life that works for you, regardless of what anyone else thinks of your choices. So me sitting here and telling you how you 'must' use the book would be counterproductive at best, and probably a tad hypocritical.

Are you ready to reclaim the Magick of You?

I'm not going to tell you that the process of identifying and then prioritising your own desires and dreams, let alone actually manifesting them, will be quick or easy. Nor will I promise you that by the time you've finished this book, you'll know how to 'achieve your heart's desire in just 30 days!!!'

This is a magickal way of *living* your life, rather than any kind of quick fix.

You'll need to consciously reject many of the messages you've been taught, either overtly or more subtly, over much of your life. You'll need to actively notice and break patterns you've probably been completely unaware of up to this point. And of course, you'll need to take regular, consistent action, day after day, week after week.

Because this kind of work very rarely happens overnight.

But what I can tell you is that almost everyone I know who's done the work has said that it's been 100% worth it. Plus, if you do it right (by which I mean 'in the right way for you'), it can also be rewarding, enjoyable and even just plain *fun*.

If you want to know where you'll be in 20 years, think about the compound effects of each of your daily choices. Do most of them move you closer to, or further away from, all the things you really want to experience over what's left of your 4,000 weeks?

As I said earlier, little things matter. So implementing the right combination of magickal habits, practices and rituals for you – however small and simple they may individually be – will help you to:

- align more fully with who you truly are at your core

- believe in and trust yourself wholeheartedly

- identify what you most want and prioritise bringing it into reality

- tap into something bigger than yourself to make your priorities happen

- feel lighter and more joyful in your everyday life

- create a greater sense of flow in your outer world

- recognise the unique gifts you can offer yourself and the world

- fully, finally, reclaim the real Magick of You

I want you to take what you learn in this book and make it completely your own. Then, once you've tailored it to the one-of-a-kind individual that you are, I want you to use it consistently, on whatever schedule works for you, to reconnect with your magick.

Finally, when you've made that connection, I want you to step into the power it brings to create the changes you dream of in your life and the world around you. Because the world needs your magick, and you're the only one who can bring it into being.

It's time to step into the creative power and beauty of who you really are. It's time to become the person you were always meant to be.

Are you ready to reclaim the Magick of You?

I'm so excited to help you discover what's waiting for you when you do!

Section 1: **Key Concepts**

Underlying concepts that will help you to
understand the foundations of your magick

1.1 What is Magick?

Magick is about creating change

Let's talk about what I mean when I use the word 'magick'. In particular, let's talk about what I mean by 'the Magick of You'.

For a start, you may wonder why I spell magick with a 'k'. I do that to show that I'm not talking about stage magicians and rabbit-in-a-hat magic.

The magick I'm talking about isn't based in entertainment, illusions or the suspension of disbelief.

Instead, magick-with-a-k is about presence. It's an internal connection to your inner power and authority. It's about taking responsibility for yourself and your actions. And, perhaps most powerfully, it's about consciously using both internal and external energy to create change in your life.

There's often fear, uncertainty and misunderstanding around what magick is. People may associate it with fantasy witches and wizards. They may think that to be magickal, they need to be born into magick, have a magickal lineage or have special skills.

Some may even associate magick with evil or harm, thanks to fairy tales and an establishment that's always feared individuals who own their power.

But magick is neutral. It's not good or bad. It just *is*.

Each person decides how they'll wield and weave their energies – their magick – in the world. You get to choose whether you'll use your magick to create change that supports you and the world around you... or if you'll do the opposite.

Dion Fortune, a very influential figure in the birth of Modern Witchcraft, described magick as, "the art of changing consciousness at will."

We get to create so much of our experience of life, and we do most of it unconsciously, not realising the power we have to create change.

The role of spells (AKA confirmation bias)

If you want to create change in your life or the way you experience the world, you need to embody your magick. And the good news is that doing that is simpler than you might think.

You don't need any special equipment or sacred tools. You don't even need to know which phase the moon is in (although yes, that's fun).

But you *do* need to be aware of spells, and not spells as in hocus pocus or 'double double toil and trouble'.

Instead, I'm talking about spells in the form of words.

Every day, you 'cast spells' with your words and thoughts. Whenever you think that something will work out or fail, you subtly direct your energy towards that outcome. Every thought you have and every word you speak helps to cast a spell.

Henry Ford famously said, "Whether you think you can, or you think you can't – you're right."

He was right too. When you strongly believe something, you either consciously or unconsciously direct your energy and use your magick to create a spell that supports your belief.

We all do this all the time. In psychology, it's called confirmation bias: our tendency to process information by looking for, and interpreting, whatever aligns with our already-held beliefs.

No doubt you've seen this in action when you believe one thing and someone else believes another. You might be surprised to find that both of you clearly see evidence to support your own views.

Confirmation bias also shows up when you're meeting people. If you meet someone that you've been told earlier is kind and considerate, you'll notice all the ways that they are kind and considerate to you.

But if that same person was introduced to a friend who'd been told to watch out for them as they were sneaky and deceitful, your friend would notice all the untrustworthy things that person did.

You might see that person's smile as warm and friendly. Yet, to your friend, it might seem sly and insincere.

One theory is that our brains do this because of a bundle of nerves called the Reticular Activating System (RAS). Your RAS helps you to filter and make sense of the huge amount of information you're presented with and immersed in each day. This filtering needs to happen, or the sheer volume of information you have to process would completely overwhelm you.

However, filtering all that information means your RAS often only provides you with evidence that validates and confirms your own existing beliefs. In other words: your beliefs tell your RAS which information to give you.

So, if you think you're bad at something, your RAS will only show you the information that supports that belief. However, if you think that great things will happen to you, your RAS will also seek out and show you all of the great things that you experience.

This ability to consciously choose to create change by directing your inner energy to set the conditions you desire (and then take aligned, focused action) is truly magick.

Basically, to live a more magickal life, you set your intention with a plan that could work without magick. Then, you bring your magick to make following that plan better, easier and more joyful.

Activity: **Noticing the magick that's already present**

To see your RAS in action, for the next three days, try to witness the magick that already exists in your life.

Be aware that, to start with, you may feel as if you're trying so hard to notice whatever you're supposed to pay attention to that you wonder if you're making it up.

If so, don't try to 'look' for magick. Instead, allow yourself to remain present and see what draws your attention. Throughout the day, you may realise that you've just experienced the activity without trying at all.

Recording what you notice

If you already keep an everyday journal, consider recording anything you notice in this exercise in there. If not, you may want to dedicate a special notebook to the journey of reclaiming your magick. Or you might be happy to use a plain, 'cheap and cheerful' notebook you have lying around the house. You could even use a notes app on your phone, or a digital file on your computer if you prefer.

We'll talk more about the great 'paper and pen vs digital' journaling debate in *Chapter 4.3 – Soul Vitamin Habits* when we look at journaling in more depth.

For now, though, whatever you like working in is fine: it's the act of writing your thoughts down that matters.

Day 1. Experiencing joy

On the first day, set an intention to experience or witness more joy throughout your day. Be open to the joy showing up in different ways. For example, you might:

- experience something intensely joyful, or simply notice small moments of joy in your life
- witness joy in other people around you
- see the word 'joy' written in books, magazines or on a coffee cup
- overhear the word being spoken
- even meet someone called Joy

Day 2. Seeing a particular colour of feather or a specific animal

On the second day, choose the specific animal or the colour of feather you want to see, and set an intention to see it. Again, be open to how it shows up. Perhaps you'll:

- see the feather on the ground or attached to a bird
- notice the animal in a book, on your TV screen or in a meme someone sends you
- just hear someone talking about feathers or your chosen animal

Day 3. Becoming aware of synchronicities

For the final day, set the intention to notice synchronicities that pop up over the day.

To do this, you could set an alarm to remind yourself at various times throughout the day to stop what you're doing, become present and use your senses to tune into the activity. Then see what you become aware of.

Additionally, at the end of the day, you could reflect back and ask yourself:

- What happened for you that you hadn't planned?
- What did you need or want to do, that just coincidently came your way?
- How obvious or subtle were each of these discoveries?

Finally, at the end of the three days, reflect back over everything you noticed, and how things showed up most often for you.

In particular, note the sense that allowed you to become aware of whatever you'd set the intention to notice that day. Did you see the magick? Hear it? Touch it?

We'll talk a lot about your senses in future chapters, and this exercise will give you a head start on identifying what your dominant sense might be.

Magick and power

Magick is a powerful tool that we can use to create incredible positive change in the world. Yet many of us still deny it, doubt it or distrust it.

This is often a reflection of the relationship we have with ourselves.

Once we start to recognise that we can create change in our lives, and that we're not just victims of old stories or situations, we start to realise how truly powerful we are.

However, it can be extremely challenging to recognise that, even as just one person, we can create significant change in the world. Part of the reason for this is that if we accept that we have the ability to make something better, we can feel like we have a *responsibility* to do so. So sometimes, it can just be easier and more comfortable to believe we have no power to change anything.

Another part is that we can often have a distorted connection to the idea of power that makes us want to avoid it. We think about how we've seen power modelled to us, and it's usually a controlling, reckless, even abusive power. We learn to fear power, because we've seen the pain it can cause when it's used to manipulate, dominate or control.

But the power you connect to as you embody your magick is an inner power, and it's something completely different. It's quiet, steady and present – not loud or demanding.

This is a power from within. It's the power to create, the power to have faith in the unseen, and the power to connect with and trust your intuition.

This type of power is often seen as a connection to the mysteries of life and the darkness of the unknown.

We've always been taught to fear the dark. It's where the monsters live... but it's also exactly where your power resides.

When you can tap into the creative, intuitive, powerful energy within, you start to become aware of how you actually show up in the world.

You start to recognise your own needs and desires. You become aware of both the creative and the destructive spells you've been casting.

And as you become more in tune with yourself, you start to recognise and tap into the rhythms that flow around and within you. When this happens, you can use your knowledge and experience of those rhythms to create change or influence the world around you.

It won't always be comfortable

As you start to embody the Magick of You, it's normal for doubts to creep in.

You're changing. Or, in a truer sense, you're releasing what wasn't yours to begin with and letting go of what you've outgrown that no longer serves or supports you.

It's a process that reveals more of the truth of who you are at your core.

You might think that this would be easy. Surely, once you began to remember your magick, you'd embrace it with joy? But it's human nature to resist change.

Our current experience of life is familiar. We might not always like what we experience. We may *want* something different. If we stay the same, though, at least we know what to expect.

There's a comfort and a safety in that.

Choosing a new path – a life of magick – can feel hard. It can even feel risky because it's new. When we do something new, we don't know what to expect or where it will lead.

And as if our own inner resistance wasn't hard enough, the people around us often resist us changing too.

I like to think of making these changes as being like going to the gym (yes, we're at the gym again!)

When you go to the gym and use weights to get stronger, healthier muscles, you don't just build those muscles out of nothing. The exercise you do actually damages some of your existing muscle fibres.

Then, in the process of recovering from the exercise during the rest period that follows, your body heals these muscle fibres and grows them back. And they grow back stronger, so they can cope with the new stress they find themselves under.

You go to the gym, work out, and perhaps the next day or the day after that, your muscles feel sore. Maybe you struggle to sit down after doing some great squats.

To support your journey of getting stronger, you don't swear off the gym forever more, though. (Well, you might, but you don't mean it.) Instead, you take it easy for a bit. You might do some gentle stretches, or perhaps have a massage or an Epsom salts bath to relax.

I want you to start thinking of embodying your magick the same way. Just like your squats 'break down' existing muscle fibres, as you connect with and embody your magick, you're breaking down old judgements and stories. You're 'regrowing' new beliefs and priorities so you can become stronger in your sense of yourself.

You may feel discomfort, just like when you've gone hard on your squats. But instead of giving up on your magick, I want you to support yourself the same way you'd support your aching leg muscles.

Take it slowly. Be kind to yourself. Get some more sleep, get a massage or have a bath.

Because just like with your aching muscles, it's uncomfortable. The good news is that it's also a sign that you've been training and making progress. It's something you can feel proud of. Plus, you know it's only temporary.

In just the same way, feel the discomfort with your magick. Know that it will pass, and be proud that you're beginning to choose yourself, and your own desires and priorities.

In both cases, you need to get comfortable with the discomfort. You need to lean into it, knowing that without it, none of the growth and magick can happen. And in both cases, you come out stronger and fitter.

Of course, if the doubts feel overwhelming, it's also important to be able to 'listen through them'. You might never fully silence them, or the judgements and expectations from both yourself and those around you. What you *can* do is at least dial them down enough to hear, trust and interpret your inner-most wisdom and guidance: your intuition.

So what *is* intuition? Let's take an in-depth look at exactly what it is and isn't – and the vital role it plays in the process of reclaiming the Magick of You.

Key insights to take with you

- Although magick is often feared or even ridiculed, it's simply about consciously using your energy and inner power to create change.

- Living a more magickal life is about setting an intention via a plan that would work without magick... then using magick to make following the plan easier and more joyful.

- We often learn to distrust power because it's been modelled to us as controlling, dominating and manipulative, but inner power is very different to this.

- Much like going to the gym to get stronger, strengthening your magick is a process that isn't always comfortable, but the discomfort is part of the growth.

A question to think about

What aspects of your inner power are you already comfortable connecting with? What still feels uncomfortable and untrustworthy?

1.2 The Role of Intuition

What is intuition?

As you reconnect with and reclaim the Magick of You, you become more confident in knowing what you want and need. You start to honour your needs and choices more. Some of these choices may not make logical sense, but they *feel* right, and you begin to trust yourself and this inner knowing more.

You also start to make decisions based on what you know to be true or right for you, and not just based on logic or reason.

That's why part of reclaiming the Magick of You is becoming more connected to the inner wisdom and guidance within you: your intuition.

I define intuition as 'your immediate, often unexplained, understanding of something'.

You might call this 'trusting your gut', 'tuning into your sixth sense' or 'listening to your feelings'.

Regardless of the name, it's that quiet voice whose message you just *know* to be true when it speaks to you. Maybe it's a whisper, or a feeling pulling you forward. Or perhaps it's the quiet voice that encourages you to make the changes you desire, or that gently tells you to try again.

Your intuition usually comes as a moment of clarity or a deep, immediate knowing about something that you can't logically explain.

Maybe you can remember a time when you walked into a room and just knew that something wasn't right. No one said anything wrong, and nothing looked obviously out of place... but you just knew. Or perhaps you felt a strong internal call to follow a certain desire, and instantly *knew* that it was what you needed to do next in your life.

A few years ago, I interviewed Becky Walsh, who said that we have two types of intuition: heart intuition and gut intuition.

Heart intuition is what pulls us forward. It shows us whether actions are or aren't aligned for us. Perhaps you feel this kind of intuition as a deep knowing that it's time to change jobs, start a new career or leave a relationship.

Meanwhile, gut intuition moves us back and away from danger. You might experience this kind of intuition when you meet someone who just feels 'off', or get a sense that you shouldn't walk down a certain road. That's your gut intuition keeping you safe.

Regardless of the form it takes, intuition is a type of inner wisdom and guidance that complements your intellectual, logical reasoning.

And it's almost impossible to connect to and embody your magick without factoring intuitive guidance into the process.

Not every internal voice is your intuition

Of course, sometimes the messages from the voices in your head *aren't* helpful ones.

Maybe your inner voice insists that you've done something wrong (again), that you're (still) not good enough or that you don't deserve what you desire (and never will).

Or perhaps it insists that something you feel a soul calling to do is far too dangerous and would never work out, even though you know intellectually that it's safe.

The examples in the previous section were your intuition communicating with you. The voices above in this section are – respectively – your inner critic and your trauma-based fear speaking.

How can you tell which is which?

You tell by paying attention to the quality of the messages you receive.

Intuition is subtle and nuanced. Its messages are generally quiet, and either emotionally neutral or gently encouraging. Usually, the quieter and easier to overlook the information you receive is, the more you can trust it.

If you feel highly charged emotions when you receive your guidance, that's probably not your intuition. Instead, it's likely to be a reflexive reaction to past experiences that you've been through.

Your body stores the memory of any trauma you've experienced. Then, whenever you encounter a situation that reminds you of that first traumatic experience, your body goes into protection mode. It sends out alarm signals, warning you that the new situation isn't safe. This can hold you back from trying new experiences and stretching beyond your comfort zone.

If, on the other hand, the guidance you receive involves negative messages about yourself or someone else, it's your inner critic. The same is true if the guidance feels like you're being told off.

Either way, whether it's your trauma or your inner critic speaking, you don't need to listen.

Activity: **Identifying your intuition when it speaks**

To differentiate between what is and isn't your intuition, you need to get to know yourself really well.

Doing this starts with learning to regulate your nervous system, which can be as simple as giving yourself a moment to take a breath.

When you feel something that might be your intuition, notice the sensation you feel.

- Where do you feel it in your body?
- How emotionally charged does it (and do you) feel?

If you feel charged, take a couple of slow, deep breaths and exhale fully. Then, simply witness whatever's going on for you. Get present in your body, and let yourself breathe through the feeling.

Close your eyes, put your hand on your heart and remind yourself that you're safe.

How do you feel now?

Keep a record

As with recording what you noticed in the previous chapter's exercise, an important way to help you differentiate your intuition from other voices is to keep a record of how your past intuitive nudges have played out. Again, you can do this however you like, but whatever you use, start to record every internal nudge or feeling that you think might be your intuition communicating with you.

Note down how the message felt, where you felt it in your body and whether it was accompanied by any emotion.

Keeping this kind of record will help you to clearly understand how stored trauma, fear and your actual intuition each feel in your body. As a result, you'll learn to untangle the voices of each, and clearly know which one you're listening to.

Coming to your senses

I mentioned in the activity in *Chapter 1.1 – What is Magick?* that you might notice magick showing up in your life via a dominant sense. Your intuition too often communicates with you through your dominant sense, assuming you have one.

We'll go into much more detail about how to identify your dominant sense later in *Chapter 4.3 – Soul Vitamin Habits*. For the meantime, to get a feel for what sense this might be for you, think about how you'd like to spend your perfect day. Is there a dominant sense that you'd choose to indulge?

- If you'd get a luxurious massage or go for a walk in nature with the sun on your face, your dominant sense might be feeling.

- If you'd visit an art gallery or watch a sunset, your dominant sense might be vision.

- If you'd listen to your favourite music at home or attend a concert, your dominant sense might be hearing.

Equally, think about which sense is the quickest to get overwhelmed for you.

- If everything just feels too intense and overwhelming, your dominant sense might be feeling.

- If lights suddenly become too bright or colours start to clash with each other, your dominant sense might be vision.

- If your surroundings become too loud and certain noises start to grate on your awareness, your dominant sense might be hearing.

If you notice that you do have one dominant sense, pay more attention to the intuitive information you receive through that channel.

For example, you might get a feeling in the pit of your stomach when you think about something. Or maybe you see an image or a sign, or have a flash of inspiration. Perhaps you hear a clear message or overhear a few words from a song or passing conversation.

Regardless, note down what you noticed, and anything that happened afterwards. If you accepted it as an intuitive message and took action based on it, what was the outcome? And if you didn't, what was the outcome of that?

Whatever you decided, don't make yourself wrong for it. You're effectively learning a completely new language – the language your body and intuition use to communicate with you. It's natural to make mistakes and interpret a cue wrong sometimes.

Let your intuition come to you

Unfortunately, our culture doesn't teach us to listen to intuition. Instead, it teaches us to dismiss intuitive messages in various ways, for example...

- We can doubt ourselves by overthinking a situation and listening to other people's (many) opinions.

- Unconscious biases, assumptions and judgements can drown out our intuitive wisdom.

- 'Should's and expectations can make us want to avoid causing a fuss, disappointing others or letting them down.

- The desire for an opportunity, person or status can be bigger and louder than our intuitive voices.

- Previous trauma can disconnect us from our own experiences, leaving us distrusting ourselves and any intuitive messages.

Many years ago, someone asked outdoor survival expert Ray Mears how to get the most out of their upcoming trip to the jungle.

His response has always stayed with me. He said, and I'm paraphrasing, "Walk into the jungle and stop. Let the jungle come to you."

I just love that for so many reasons. It's true for the jungle, and it's also true for your intuition. If you try too hard or go stomping too loud, you'll scare everything you're hoping to see and experience in the jungle away. But when you take a moment to stop, to get silent and still, you let the jungle (and your intuition) come to you.

But listening to your intuition is just part of the process of connecting to and reclaiming the Magick of You. In *Chapter 1.1 – What is Magick?*, we also briefly talked about the role that energy – both your internal energy, and the energy of the world around you – play in embodying your magick.

So next, we're going to talk more about what energy is, and why it's so important to learn to manage yours wisely.

Key insights to take with you

- I define intuition as 'your immediate, often unexplained, understanding of something'.

- It generally comes as a moment of clarity or a deep, immediate knowing about something that you can't logically explain.

- Not all of the internal voices you hear will be your intuition: sometimes they might be your inner critic or your trauma-based fear.

- The voice of your intuition is usually quiet, calm and either neutral or gently encouraging.

- Learning to differentiate the voice of your intuition from other internal voices often takes practice and a willingness to get it wrong sometimes.

A question to think about

What are some situations where you've listened to a voice you thought was your intuition in the past? What did that voice sound like, and what happened afterwards?

1.3 Understanding Energy

Everything you experience affects your energy

One of the most significant factors in reclaiming the Magick of You is your ability to distinguish what's yours and what's not. To embody the ideas and practices outlined in this book, you need a very clear understanding of what comes from within you, and what you've picked up and accepted as real from the outside world.

When I talk about what's yours, I mean everything that shapes your experience of reality, but particularly your:

- emotions and feelings
- desires
- values
- beliefs
- judgements

However, especially when you're new to the concept, it can be incredibly difficult to tease out what comes from your intuition, and what you're absorbing from:

- the people around you
- the media you consume
- the culture you live in

You do need to learn to separate them out, though. That's because, as I said back in the Introduction, everything you surround yourself with and everything you consume impacts the quality of your energy. If that energy isn't supportive, it can create a kind of 'energetic smog' that we'll talk about in more detail later in the chapter.

It doesn't matter whether you're doing the consuming consciously or unconsciously – willingly or unwillingly. Unless you actively take steps to become aware of what you're allowing in, and consciously decide whether or not you want that thing to affect you... it will.

When you're not clear on your energetic, physical, intellectual and emotional boundaries (more on those in *Chapter 3.3 – The Intentional MIND mindset*), it becomes easy to lose touch with your sense of self. You can disconnect from your own reality and what's important to you as the energy, needs and desires of those around you start to swallow you up.

Perhaps that's why so many people find such deep inner peace when they spend time in nature. It gives them a chance to connect with their true inner nature, instead of being influenced and bombarded by everything around them.

Activity: Getting a sense of your own energy

When I use the word 'energy' in this activity, I'm talking about your life force – the invisible force that flows through you and influences your body, mind and spirit.

This energy isn't associated with any particular religion or spiritual practice. However, people who work with this energy often feel a deeper sense of connection to themselves and to something greater than themselves.

Many ancient healing traditions include a concept of this kind of energy. It's called *prana* in Ayurvedic medicine, and *chi* in Traditional Chinese Medicine. If you've never physically experienced your own energy before, here are three practical exercises to help you 'feel into' it and get a sense of it for yourself.

As with previous activities, record what you did and everything you notice in a journal or notebook, or in whatever format works best for you.

1. Energy boundaries

This exercise helps you to feel the edges of your energy field as a physical sensation.

Hold your hands around a metre apart from each other, with your palms facing inwards.

Close your eyes and notice whether you can feel anything between them.

Move your hands a little closer, then stop for a few moments to see whether you become aware of your energy. You might feel it as a pulse, as a small magnetic pull or as heat or tingling in your hands and fingers.

If you don't feel anything, that's OK. Just move your hands a little closer again, then stop and check again.

Keep moving them closer and stopping, and see when you become aware of your energy.

Whenever you notice it, make a note of what you feel. Then stop and rest.

And if you don't notice anything at all at any point, that's OK too. Just try again at a later time – 'letting the jungle come to you' works with energy as well as intuition.

Shake your hands gently with your fingers loose to reset the energy in your hands.

2. Creating an energy ball

This exercise helps to fine-tune your ability to sense your own energy.

Repeat the energy boundaries exercise. But this time, when your hands are about 20cm apart, just hold them there.

Imagine you're now holding a ball of energy between your hands.

Feel the energy in the ball getting stronger and becoming more powerful.

After a minute or so of doing this, start to focus on your breath.

As you inhale, feel the energy in your hands become stronger.

As you exhale, feel the energy leaving your hands.

When you can clearly feel the energy, start to move your hands back and forth. See if you can feel the energy change as your hands move.

If you push your hands closer together, does the energy feel denser?

As you pull your hands further apart, can you feel the energy stretch?

Again, write down whatever you notice.

3. Playing with the energy ball

When you're comfortable with that exercise, fine-tune your energy sense even further by telling the ball what to do.

Hold the ball of energy in your hands once more.

Keeping your hands 20cm apart, tell your energy ball to feel heavier and denser.

Next, tell it to move to your left hand and then to your right.

Practise directing your energy with your intention.

And again, write down your experiences and whatever you notice.

Finally, when you've finished the exercise, place your hands over your stomach and feel yourself re-absorbing your energy.

Shake your hands with your fingers loose to reset and clear any excess energy.

Practise these three exercises regularly to deepen your sense of, and connection with, your own energy.

Navigating energetic smog

Earlier in the chapter, we talked about distinguishing what's yours from what isn't. And we described everything that isn't yours and that doesn't support or serve you as a kind of energetic smog around you.

That smog is there because, every day, you're in contact with people and the world. You interact with family, friends, colleagues, acquaintances and neighbours. You scroll through social media, watch the news and learn what's going on politically. Perhaps you experience conflict, or have uncomfortable conversations with others. You may have arguments or disagreements.

Regardless, every time someone offloads all their angst onto you, you can take it on in your energetic system. The same thing happens when they share their fears and concerns, or when you witness or experience a trauma or tragedy, or simply read a worrying news article.

It can even occur when someone asks for your advice on dealing with a problem.

Additionally, we're all constantly surrounded by judgements, negative opinions, disempowering thoughts, media and advertising, movies, shows and social media. And of course, most of us own all kinds of devices that encourage us to scroll excessively, keeping us immersed in these influences.

Then, on top of ALL of this, the world bombards us with messages about who we should be, what we should do, how we should spend our time and what we should accomplish.

Together, all of these interactions and experiences create that energetic smog of external thoughts, feelings, fears, judgements and opinions.

The smog can make it impossible to clearly see what belongs to you and what belongs to other people. This, in turn, can leave you uncertain about what you really want, and what you are and aren't comfortable doing to make it happen.

Unconscious energy exchanges

In addition to the energetic smog, you can sometimes end up actively exchanging energy with the people and situations around you.

For example, I'm sure you've experienced the feeling of having a great day until someone who isn't comes along, and all they want to do is moan. Then, after they leave, you just feel drained.

Or maybe you watch a film, and even though you know it's just a story, you still find yourself angry at the injustice that one of the characters experiences. Many years ago, I watched *Into the Wild*, which had such a sad ending that I physically felt off for hours after the film finished.

This happens because every time we interact with someone or something – even if it's fictional – we exchange energy with it, creating an energetic connection.

Some of those connections are tiny, with very little emotional charge. Perhaps someone holds a door open for you and you thank them.

The energetic 'cord' from this kind of exchange would be smaller than the thickness of a single hair, and would naturally dissolve as the day went on. You might not even remember it a couple of days later.

But some energetic connections are far more substantial, and create a stronger emotional charge. For example, if you have a major disagreement with someone, the energetic exchange and resulting connection will be much more significant.

Think of *these* energetic cords as massive data cables that send and receive information between you and the person you're connected to.

This kind of exchange can be a positive thing. If someone loves and supports you, you can receive that love and support through your connection with them. However, the opposite is also true: people can project their fears and judgements along the cord, and you can pick up on them.

Some of the things you might notice in yourself after this kind of unsupportive energetic exchange include:

- doubting yourself

- making a decision and then changing your mind

- not following through with things you want to achieve

- doing what you think you *should* do or what you're expected to do, instead of what's truly important to you

- playing a particular role, rather than being your true self

You might also find yourself feeling:

- like you're taking three steps forwards and then stumbling two steps back

- drained, as though someone (sometimes called an 'energy vampire' or 'emotional vampire') has siphoned off all your energy

- overwhelmed and generally not like yourself

- sudden changes in your mood or emotions

Energetic hygiene to the rescue

Back when I first started my kinesiology training in 1999, the tutor recommended a particular Psychic Protection class. The teacher for that class described picking up on other people's energy in this way:

> *"Imagine you're a farmer who's been out in the fields and mucking out the animals all day. When you come home in your muddy boots and dirty overalls, do you sit on the couch straight away? Of course not – that would be ridiculous! It would leave mud and muck all over your home, so it just doesn't make sense. And your energetic health is the same way, except that you don't see the mud."*

I wasn't really into the idea of 'psychic' anything at the time, but I went along to the class anyway. And that training was probably some of the most valuable of my life, because it started my interest in, and research into, energetic hygiene.

And gradually, as I learnt more about the topic, I became more aware of how other people interacted with my energy, and how I used my own energy with them. I grew more conscious about how I interacted with others, and started to take responsibility for how I showed up – not only in life, but in relationships too. I also learnt to take responsibility for my past decisions and actions, and take greater responsibility for my choices moving forward.

If I felt drained or depleted around certain people, I gradually learnt how to clear those feelings, and come back into my own energy. And with time, I even stopped allowing others to drain or deplete my energy. Instead, I began to quickly recognise that depletion was imminent, and protect my energy by setting more effective energetic and physical boundaries.

Learning about energetic hygiene taught me to understand where my energy ended in the world, and where other people's began. Whenever I noticed an intense emotion, I could quickly distinguish whether it was mine, or if I was picking it up from someone else or the collective energy around me.

And the techniques I learnt worked! Even after 20+ years of working energetically with thousands of clients, I never pick up anyone else's stuff now, much less keep it with me.

This makes staying connected to my magick, my values and the things that are important to me much easier. External energy rarely knocks me off track or overwhelms me these days.

Now, don't get me wrong. I'm highly intuitive, and have many 'clairs'. That's my word for a finely tuned sense that goes beyond the physical. Think clairvoyance for clear-seeing, or clairaudience for clear-hearing. And I can still use my clairs appropriately when I want to.

That's how I know that even if you're as sensitive as I am to the world around you, good energetic hygiene will help you to remain true to your own energy. It will help you to avoid undue influence from everything external, no matter how intense it may be.

The purple bubble technique

One of the most powerful techniques I know for keeping everyone else's energy and expectations out, and my own energy in, is something I call 'the purple bubble technique'.

This literally involves surrounding yourself and your energy system with a beautiful purple bubble of energy. You don't have to be able to feel or see this bubble. You just need to set the intention and then know that it's there.

I recommend using purple because it's associated with an energy that's known as the Violet Flame of transmutation. The Violet Flame has traditionally been used to transmute energies that don't belong to you and restore your own natural energy.

Using this technique means that if anything comes your way that doesn't serve you, the bubble simply transmutes it for the highest good of all involved. No drama – it's just gone. And anything that *is* yours and *does* serve you just comes straight through the bubble, cleansed and cleared to nourish and support you.

I like to think of the purple bubble as an energetic immune system. It creates a clear boundary – a barrier between what's yours and what's not. It allows in nourishment, and keeps out anything that may cause you harm or discomfort.

It's a bit like breathing too, in that you don't need to constantly think about your purple bubble for it to work. Whenever you bring your attention to it, though, it becomes much more effective.

As you practise visualising your bubble, you may want to change aspects of it. Here are a few things to think about playing with.

What size is your bubble?

Your purple bubble probably won't be static. Just like a real bubble, it will change and move – shifting size and position gently around you.

Visualising your bubble isn't about creating an iron shield to hide behind and block all of life out. It's about connecting with the energy of a living, breathing bubble, and allowing that energy to communicate with you and respond to what you need.

Some days, you might want your bubble super snug and close to you, to keep you feeling safe and cosy. On other days, that closeness might feel claustrophobic and restrictive, so you'll want to expand it to allow you to feel expansive as well.

Your bubble size might also depend on where you're planning to be that day. I live in the countryside, so I'm used to having a lot of physical space around me. When I go into the city, I keep my bubble quite close to me because I don't want everyone walking through it.

As you go through your day, you might find your bubble's size needs to change too. You might start off with a really big, expansive bubble, then want to pull it in closer to you throughout the day. Or the opposite could be true.

Keep playing around with different sizes for your bubble to find out what works for you in each situation.

What texture does it have?

I love the softness and playfulness of a real-life soap bubble, but you can create different textures for your energetic bubble depending on what you need at a given time.

For example, if you're about to have a difficult conversation or you feel a little uneasy about an upcoming event, you might want to feel a bit more protected.

In these situations, I like to imagine adding a layer of flexible purple paint to the outside of my bubble with a paintbrush or a roller brush. I set the intention of covering my whole body, including the areas that often get neglected like the soles of my feet, my back and the top of my head.

But, as with everything in this book, do whatever works for you. A friend who needed extra protection for something they had coming up once told me, "Rebecca, I'm using a cement mixer and trowel today." That imagery always makes me chuckle!

Some days, you too might need really thick, strong boundaries. On those days, get out your trowel and clearly define your edges as you go out into the world.

Does the bubble have any other colours?

You can also play with adding colours to your bubble.

If you're feeling a bit low in energy, try putting a layer of red around the outside of your purple bubble. Then take a moment to notice whether the red makes you feel energised and ready to go... or if it's so intense that it makes you uncomfortable. If the red doesn't feel good, imagine washing it off and replacing it with orange. Maybe that makes you feel joyful and a bit more positive?

Keep playing with different colours to see how each one makes you feel.

When you know what works for you, you might call in different colours for different days. For example:

- Traditionally, red is energising, but that might not always be true for you.

- Some shades of green might feel peaceful, while others might feel quite icky.

- Blue might feel calming or too cold.

- Dark navy is a very protective colour for me, and it can help me to feel invisible on the days I don't want to be seen.

- Maybe some days you'll want a rainbow or polka dots or green tartan.

Be open and curious as you explore how you feel when your bubble is 'wearing' different colours. Eventually, you'll know exactly which colour you need the moment you wake up and feel a particular way.

But regardless of the colour you use for your outer layer, always start with a basic bubble of purple for protection and to tap into that energy of transmutation.

Energetic hygiene in context

Finally, it's important to recognise that a key part of creating good energetic hygiene is to get really clear on what's important to you.

This isn't just about knowing in the moment which individual feelings, judgements and opinions are yours and which aren't. It's also about the biggest possible picture:

- What are your most important priorities for your life?

- What are your core, non-negotiable values?

- What practical direction do you want to take your life in?

Or, as Mary Oliver so beautifully put it in her poem *A Summer Day*, "What is it you plan to do with your one wild and precious life?"

These are the sorts of questions that can take time and regular deep connection with yourself and your inner knowing to figure out. Or, occasionally, the answers might arrive in a sudden, immediate flash of insight – but remember that not every internal voice you hear is your intuition. So if you experience this kind of intuitive flash, don't forget to pay attention to its quality, the way we discussed in *Chapter 1.2 – The Role of Intuition*.

To help you start navigating these questions, we're going to talk about how to create your own Magickal Life Philosophy in the next section. We'll also talk about using a magickal mindset, magickal habits and magickal practices in Sections 3, 4 and 5 to help keep your energy running clear and free of unhelpful external influences.

And for more help with improving your energetic hygiene specifically, keep an eye out for the GRACE practice in *Section 5: Magickal Practices*.

Together, these techniques will help you to focus on creating the life you desire as you reconnect with and reclaim the Magick of You.

Key insights to take with you

- Everything you experience affects the quality of your energy, which in turn affects the quality of your magick.

- The thoughts, opinions, values and judgements of other people, along with social media, advertising, news and more create a kind of energetic smog around you.

- To help you differentiate what's yours from what isn't, you need a clear sense of your own energetic boundaries.

- One technique that can help you to maintain those boundaries is the purple bubble technique, which you can customise to your needs at any given moment.

A question to think about

Where does most of the energetic smog in your life come from right now? Can you easily limit or remove any of the sources?

Section 2: Your Magickal Life Philosophy

Creating a life philosophy that supports you in reclaiming
and reconnecting with your magick

2.1 Understanding Your Magickal Life Philosophy

Knowing what you want isn't always easy

Often, when I ask someone what they want from life, they can tell me all the things they want for other people they're close to. But somehow, they completely leave themselves out.

When I ask again, and specify that I'm asking what *they* actually want for themselves, people often get confused. They might discover they're not really sure. Sometimes, they feel upset and even angry, as they realise that they have no idea of the answer.

Maybe that sounds familiar?

The problem is that, just like with the car in the Introduction, if you simply drive without knowing where you're heading, you could end up anywhere.

Sometimes the question of what you want can seem too big, with too many available options and so many more that you may not even be aware of.

Deciding on what you want can feel overwhelming. What if you get it wrong, or head down the wrong path?

Having too many choices can also trap you in a state of not knowing, sometimes referred to as analysis paralysis.

This is where developing a supportive life philosophy can help.

What is a life philosophy?

A life philosophy is your general attitude to, and outlook on, life. It's like a set of rules that you choose to live by, and make all your choices to act according to. A life philosophy often contains two aspects:

- your beliefs about how the world is governed at a spiritual level, and

- what you value at a personal level, which then dictates how you want to show up in the world

We all have a philosophy for life, although we may not be conscious of what it is.

Many of us inherit ours from the people we grew up with. We never question it, instead accepting it as 'just the way the world is.' Then we see everything we experience in life through the unconscious lens of our philosophy.

Philosophies can empower us, perhaps sounding like:

- You're the author of your own life.

- Life is short. Do what makes you happy.

- Life is full of beauty, awe and wonder.

- Follow your heart.

- Everything works out in the end.

Or they can disconnect us from our power, and sound more like:

- Life is hard.
- It's a dog-eat-dog world.
- There's no point in trying – I can't make a difference anyway.
- You have to be practical. Dreaming just leads to disappointment.
- Nothing ever works out for me.

Reclaiming and embodying the Magick of You requires intentionally creating a life philosophy that focuses on and celebrates all that is you. And, as I mentioned in the Introduction, that means all of you, not just the pretty, socially acceptable parts.

Society has conditioned us to think that we're both 'not enough' and at the same time 'too much' if we speak out or express ourselves fully. A supportive life philosophy can help to counter this, by focusing us on what we want to do and become, regardless of anyone else's views on the topic.

My personal life philosophy

My own philosophy is simple: it's to remember that there's always a way. That way may not be easy or obvious, but I need to remain open and curious about finding it throughout all areas of my life, particularly during the challenges.

I know that sometimes I won't find the way, but approaching a situation as if I can makes everything feel so much more possible and less daunting.

My guiding feelings and values are joy, growth and creativity. So even when I don't find a way forward, whatever I learn along the way always proves useful, which then leads me to one of my values.

I choose to live a life filled with magick, awe and wonder. This keeps me in the energies of joy, growth and creativity, and allows me to stay open to new opportunities and experiences that I might never have thought of or noticed otherwise. It allows me to consciously respond to situations rather than react to them.

Perhaps most importantly, it fills my life with joy and fun, and anything less would simply feel boring and constrictive to me.

You get what you expect

The thoughts that you have most of the time become your beliefs, and your beliefs become what you expect – and (mostly) experience – from life.

Here's how that works. You get what you expect because your expectations strongly influence your attitude. Your attitude influences your choices. Your choices determine your actions, reactions and responses to life. And then your actions, reactions and responses create a significant amount of your experience of the world.

This isn't a one-time effect, either. Your experience of the world proves to you that your beliefs were right. So each belief becomes more ingrained as your truth, and the cycle continues.

That is, it does until you realise that you can begin to change it.

It's possible to unlearn many of the unhelpful beliefs that disconnect you from your power and your magick, and replace them with beliefs that support you.

A powerful way to identify your existing unhelpful beliefs and create supportive, affirming beliefs instead is to consciously create a Magickal Life Philosophy. I call this kind of philosophy 'magickal' because it actively connects you to your magick and power, and helps you to embody The Magick of You.

This is an overall attitude towards your life and its purpose that you consciously, deliberately choose. It's a way of seeing the world that supports who you truly are and what you want to create. More than that, it's a philosophy that reflects your *true* beliefs and values, not just the ones you think you *should* have.

If you're lacking purpose, direction, clarity or meaning in your life, it's likely that your current life philosophy isn't right for you.

Consciously choosing a Magickal Life Philosophy will give you that sense of purpose and meaning. It will allow you to respond to life and its events with clarity and conviction, rather than reacting from doubt, fear or confusion.

What do you want out of life?

As we touched on in the Introduction, we're here in our human bodies for a limited amount of time. Oliver

Burkeman reminds us that if we live to be 80, it works out as just a little under 4,000 weeks.

Similarly, Will Storr says in *The Science of Storytelling*:

> *"We know how this ends. You're going to die and so will everyone you love... but that's not how we live our lives."*

It's true. Many of us live as if we'll never die. That can be wonderful, but it can lead us to be indifferent to life too.

Instead of connecting to the magick and wonder of life, and getting laser clear on how we want to spend our relatively short, possible-4,000 weeks on Earth, we fill our lives with things that don't serve, support or inspire us.

We rarely stop to ask whether the activities we do are meaningful to us. Do they provide value, or are they simply distractions to pass the time?

So... what do you want out of life?

Do you really know?

I said earlier that a Magickal Life Philosophy gives you a sense of purpose and direction. That's because its rules provide a guiding compass, allowing you to navigate each area of your life that's important to you. These rules also help you to commit to prioritising yourself, your desires and the particular way of being that best serves and supports you.

Your Magickal Life Philosophy helps you to design a life that aligns with what's genuinely important to you. This means you create it from a place of confidence, clarity, peace, power and purpose.

Living your Magickal Life Philosophy means you create your life with intention, in a way that supports and nourishes you.

The danger of a junk life philosophy

If you don't consciously create a Magickal Life Philosophy, you risk ending up with the opposite: a junk life philosophy.

Much of the world you live in has been deliberately designed to encourage you to neglect what's important to you. It's set up to distract you and give you the tools to numb out your feelings of discomfort.

From the time you're young, you're taught to look for wisdom outside of yourself. You're encouraged to constantly seek the counsel of celebrity 'experts' who often stand above you on a pedestal.

You're taught to trust only in reason and logic, discounting your own intuition and desires.

You're taught the goals you should have, what you should strive for, and what success should universally look like. And you're taught which values are good and virtuous, and which are bad or selfish.

Most of the things you learn from your family, society and culture have been passed down through the generations. When they get to you – if you're like most people – you just accept them without question.

After all, that's just 'the way things are'.

Our values are often based on the dreams and desires of generations long before us. As I heard Yuval Noah Harari, author of *Sapiens*, say on a podcast once, "We are trapped living the dreams of dead people."

Some of what you learn will be useful and supportive. However, it's helpful to look closely at each value, each measure of success and each philosophy you unconsciously live by. Ask yourself, "Is this mine? Do I want it? Or is this just junk for me?"

Johann Hari, author of *Lost Connections*, says that we know junk food can make us physically sick. What we might not realise is that junk values can also make us depressed. He continues:

> "Junk food looks like food, but it doesn't meet our underlying nutritional needs. In a similar way, junk values don't meet our underlying psychological needs — to have meaning and connection in our lives. Extrinsic values are KFC for the soul. Yet our culture constantly pushes us to live extrinsically."

Unless your Magickal Life Philosophy has you at the centre of it, and everything in it motivates you intrinsically, it's nothing more than a junk philosophy.

Activity: Feeling into a philosophy that supports you

One way to create your Magickal Life Philosophy is to ground it in your feelings or values.

Start with the question: if you could experience a particular feeling or value every day, what would it be? Maybe it would be joy or passion. Or perhaps honesty or adventure.

Regardless, if you could wake up each morning knowing that your day would be filled with that feeling or value, what would make you look forward to the day ahead?

You don't have to restrict yourself to just one feeling or value, either.

Whatever you choose, imagine going through your day experiencing those feelings and values.

How would it feel to experience them in your family, your relationships or your career? What about experiencing them whilst walking, enjoying your hobbies or spending time alone? Imagine using them to guide your choices and respond to the events of life.

Take a moment to let those feelings fill up your entire body. Let them grow and expand out from your heart.

As you feel them, you might want to let a gentle smile spread across your face as the experience spreads throughout your entire body.

Feel this energy of fulfilment, as you imagine what it would be like to have these emotions and values at the front and centre of every day. Feel the energy moving down your body, down through your legs and into your feet. Let yourself ground and anchor it into the floor.

Then let the energy travel out from your heart, across the front of your chest, down your arms, and gently up into your head.

Feel every cell of your body activated by everything you want to experience more of.

It doesn't matter if you don't constantly have this in your daily life right now. It's OK if you just get tiny glimpses of it once a month.

At this point, you just need to know which feelings you'd *want* to experience every day. Which life experiences would make you feel fulfilled, satisfied, nourished and nurtured? Which values could you live according to that would allow you to say, "Today was a good day," as you went to bed at night?

Don't worry if this is a bit tricky to start with. It doesn't matter if you think you're making it all up. This isn't an intellectual exercise – it's just for fun. So let your imagination run free.

Once you have a sense of the feelings and values you want at the heart of your Magickal Life Philosophy, it's time to ask yourself some questions. Again, answer these in your journal or wherever you've been recording your experiences with the activities so far.

To start with, look at the three main areas of your life philosophy.

Basic needs:

- What things do you genuinely NEED in life?
- Why do you need each of them?

Desires:

- What other things do you want in life?
- Why do you want each of them?
- Where has each want come from?
- How do you want to feel?
- Why is each particular feeling important to you?
- Where does each feeling show up in your life now?
- Where has it been absent?

Meaning:

- What makes life meaningful to you?
- What else do you think is meaningful in life?
- What do you do right now that brings meaning to your life?
- How do you want to act in relationships to make them feel more meaningful to you?

Write down your Magickal Life Philosophy

Once you've explored these questions, look for the patterns. Which themes or discoveries feel most aligned to you?

Use these themes to write out your own personal Magickal Life Philosophy.

It may just be a short sentence, like the ones at the beginning of this chapter. Or it may be paragraphs, or even pages, long. For example, your philosophy might be:

- To live a life that aligns with your power and magick, and live with integrity guiding your decisions and actions. To always look for the opportunities in life, and give yourself permission to discover what's really possible for you.

- To choose courage and boldness. To show up with the passion and willingness to choose your biggest, boldest dreams over momentary comfort, and push yourself beyond your comfort zone to achieve them.

- To believe in yourself and your ability to overcome any obstacles in your way. To be resilient and flexible in responding to life and doing what it takes to reach your dreams.

Whatever the length, honour your own process. There's no wrong way to do this – just what's right and aligned for you.

Start to embody your Magickal Life Philosophy

Once you've written down your Magickal Life Philosophy, think of six to eight important areas of your life. These could be your health, relationships, career, community, finances, hobbies, etc.

For each area, ask yourself:

- How can you live more of your Magickal Life Philosophy in that area?

- What would become true for you if you lived more of your Magickal Life Philosophy in that area?

- What benefits will you get from living more of your Magickal Life Philosophy in that area?

- How could living your Magickal Life Philosophy in that area create a greater sense of personal safety and security?

- What does it feel like to *not* live your Magickal Life Philosophy in that area?

Review your life philosophy regularly

It's important to recognise that your Magickal Life Philosophy isn't set in stone. Instead, it's natural for it to grow and evolve as you do.

So it's a good idea to review your life philosophy regularly to see if it needs refining, and if everything in it still holds true for you. I recommend putting a note in your diary or planner to remind you to check in and review it at least every six months.

Key insights to take with you

- A life philosophy is your general attitude to, and outlook on, life. It's like a set of rules or a code of conduct that you live by.

- Much like the food you eat, your life philosophy can serve and support you... but it can also act like junk food to disempower and depress you.

- Reclaiming and embodying the Magick of You requires intentionally creating a life philosophy that focuses on and celebrates all that is you.

- I call this kind of philosophy a Magickal Life Philosophy, and developing it starts with identifying the feelings and values you want to experience every single day.

A question to think about

How could having a Magickal Life Philosophy create a deeper sense of meaning and purpose in your life and help you to reconnect with your magick?

2.2 Getting Full of Yourself

Ever been told not to be too full of yourself?

Reclaiming the Magick of You requires you to honour who you are by putting yourself front and centre of your own life. It demands prioritising your own needs, your own dreams and your own values.

In essence, it asks you to become full of your own desires, so you can become full of a life that nourishes you.

In other words, you need to get 'full of yourself'.

Here in the UK, saying that someone's full of themselves is usually a criticism.

But I have a very different take on the matter. As far as I'm concerned:

YOU NEED TO BE FULL OF YOURSELF!

Now, when you read that sentence, you might find yourself reacting and judging me.

Of *course* you might.

Because, regardless of where you live, you were probably encouraged to stay small from the time you were a young child. On top of this, depending on where you grew up, you might have been told:

- not to get too big for your boots (in the UK)
- not to act above your station (in Ireland)

- not to get too big for your britches (in the US)
- not to be the tall poppy (in Australia or New Zealand)

And when I asked some friends who grew up speaking other languages about similar phrases they had in their country, I discovered they'd learnt:

- not to have swollen ankles (in France)
- not to walk next to their shoes or stick their head above ground level (in The Netherlands)
- not to be a peanut that's forgotten its skin (in Indonesia)
- not to inflate themselves with air (in Italy)
- not to grow into feathers or feather their own nest (in Poland)

No doubt every country has some kind of similar saying that encourages people to play small, and be accommodating and *selfless*.

The danger of being selfless

'Selfless' – I really hate that word! People say it as if it's some kind of virtue... but really, why on earth would you celebrate not having a self?

Surely, it's the very act of being yourself – your whole self – that makes you the incredible person you are? How can you be the fully self-expressed person you have the potential to be if you have no self to express?

Our society tends to celebrate the people, often women, who are selfless. They're the ones who can be relied on to:

- help out at school
- ferry the children around to friends, clubs or sports matches
- bake cakes for the bake sale
- look after their ageing parents
- check in on their neighbours
- always be there when a friend needs them

And they often seem to do all this while working a full-time job.

Yes, these people are indeed 'selfless'. In fact, they're usually so selfless that they've forgotten they have their own needs. They've often lost their own boundaries, and with those boundaries, their ability to say no to yet more demands.

So while society celebrates them for being selfless, they're often drained, weary and completely disconnected from any desires they once had for themselves. It's usually all they can do to make it through the day without collapsing into an exhausted heap.

Another important reason to be full of yourself is that if you're not full of your own dreams, desires and philosophy, you leave empty space in your energetic body. And since nature abhors a vacuum… that space is where other people's energetic judgements, expectations and philosophy will slip in and take residence.

As a kinesiologist, I've worked with thousands of women over 20+ years. I've noticed that the ones who try to be selfless almost never believe in or trust themselves. How can they, when they're trying so hard not to have a self to believe in or trust?

But with that loss of belief comes a disconnection from their dreams, desires, peace and inner power. The disconnection makes them a sponge for everyone else's values and expectations. Plus, as we discussed in the previous chapter, because the values they absorb aren't their own, those values are essentially 'junk' for them.

The junk values muddy the waters of their priorities, making it harder for them to remember what they want and what their own personal Magickal Life Philosophy looks like.

Have you forgotten who you are?

It's all too easy to forget who we are and what's important to us. We just somehow get caught up in the busyness of life.

Big events shape us, and we live out many roles that involve prioritising other people's needs over our own.

On top of this, we can start to identify completely with a role – maybe as a daughter, a lover, a wife, a mother, a career woman, a divorcee, a retiree… the list goes on. And each time we try to fit ourselves into the shape and expectation of the role, we lose a little more of our true essence.

Close relationships can be particularly difficult to navigate without losing your sense of self. The other person's needs can take centre stage, as you try your hardest to please them, regardless of your own feelings. Maybe you stop pursuing your own hobbies and interests to prioritise the other person and their desires.

Over time, you can actually start to lose part of your identity.

If I do this, I just become 'Rebecca, Jamie's wife', or even worse, simply 'Jamie's wife'.

Or maybe my only identity is 'Solomon's mum'. Or 'Head of the Department'.

You might initially feel happy about choosing to change your identity in this way. Or it might have happened without you noticing. Either way though, each time you identify yourself fully with a role, it can chip away a little bit more of your own unique, rich and complex sense of identity.

And that's what can happen in a fairly healthy relationship!

Unfortunately, many of the relationships people have with family members, friends or their romantic partners *aren't* healthy. In these relationships, the other person actively (whether consciously or not) undermines their relationship partner's sense of self.

Restoring a strong sense of self allows you to embody your truth, which in turn helps you to remember who you are and what's important to you.

Knowing who you are and honouring this means being aware of, and respecting, your own values, beliefs, priorities, boundaries, emotions, habits, relationships, personality and body.

It means really understanding your strengths and weaknesses without judgement. And it means being aware of all of your passions, dreams, desires, fears, quirks, likes and dislikes.

How do you like your eggs?

In the 1999 film *Runaway Bride,* Julia Roberts plays Maggie, a woman with a history of leaving men at the altar on her wedding day.

Ike (played by Richard Gere), interviews a string of Maggie's former fiancés, and among the questions he asks them is how Maggie liked her eggs cooked.

Each man has a different response, but there's a common thread to their answers. One says, "Scrambled, just like me." Another replies, "Poached, just like me." A third says, "Fried, just like me."

In every relationship, Maggie seemed to have liked her eggs exactly the same way her partner did.

Later in the movie, Ike confronts Maggie, saying, "You were so lost, you didn't even know what kind of eggs you liked! With the priest, you wanted scrambled. With the deadhead, it was fried. With the other guy, it was poached..."

Maggie tries to insist that she was just changing her mind, but Ike replies, "No, that's called not having a mind of your own."

So how do you like *your* eggs?

For all the reasons we've talked about above, even if it doesn't feel comfortable right now, you need to give yourself permission to become full of yourself.

Allow yourself to take up space with ALL of you: your thoughts, feelings, dreams, desires and physicality.

You've already asked yourself a couple of essential questions to uncover your truth when you created your Magickal Life Philosophy. But I want you to ask those questions again, and if you skipped over that part in the last chapter, here's your reminder to answer them:

- What values are important to you?
- What feelings do you want front and centre of your day?

Your honest answers to these two questions will reveal who you truly are.

If you're struggling...

The problem many people have with these questions is that it's easy to choose what they think are the *right* answers, rather than the ones that are true for them. Sometimes, their true answers are buried so deeply under layers of expectations and conditioning that it can be hard to access them.

If that's the case for you, here are a few other questions to play with. They may seem silly, but they're designed to bypass your logical, rational mind, and instead dive deep into your truth.

For each question below, write down the first answer that pops into your mind, even if it doesn't make sense. Trust that it's the right answer for you. If you overthink this exercise, it won't work.

- If you were an animal, what kind of animal would you be?

- If you were a flower, what type of flower would you be?

- If you were a colour, what colour would you be?

- If you were a biscuit (AKA a cookie if you're North American), what type would you be?

- If you were a season, what season would you be?

- If you were a pizza topping, what pizza topping would you be?

- If you were a tree, what kind of tree would you be?

- If you were a clothing item, what type of clothing would you be?

- If you were a piece of fruit, what kind of fruit would you be?

- If you were a book, what genre of book would you be?

- If you were a film, what genre of film would you be?

- If you were a restaurant, what kind of restaurant would you be?

- If you were a crystal, what kind of crystal would you be?

Go deeper and search for the themes

Now look at each of your answers and consider what it reflects about your truest self. For each answer, ask yourself:

- how you feel about it
- what it reminds you of
- what it represents to you
- what memory you associate with it

Each answer will give you a little more insight into what's important to you.

You may even notice common themes coming up for you.

For example, if you thought of a lion and a sunflower for your first two answers, perhaps your theme is being braver and bolder. Or maybe it's taking up more space with your thoughts and ideas.

Or, if you thought of a dog and a dandelion, perhaps your theme is being loyal to yourself and valuing your dreams, even if the world rejects them as a weed. (A dandelion is classed as a weed, but it's also a valuable herb with many medicinal benefits.)

You probably won't become full of yourself overnight. But you might gradually start to notice the places where you *aren't* full of your own hopes, dreams and desires – and that's a powerful start.

Once you notice the old stories and patterns, you can start to unravel them. You can begin to create space to re-write your own stories and consciously choose how you want to respond to life, rather than react. You can start to hear the voice of your intuition and make choices that are right for you and that align with your Magickal Life Philosophy, rather than ones that harm you.

As you fill yourself with what's important to you, you begin the process of reclaiming and embodying the Magick of You.

Key insights to take with you

- Our society celebrates people who are selfless, but you can't trust or believe in yourself if you don't have a self to trust or believe in.

- Similarly, we're taught that being full of ourselves is bad – but being empty creates a vacuum where everyone else's beliefs, judgements and values slip in.

- Even in healthy relationships, it's easy to stop prioritising your own needs and desires, and unhealthy relationships can increase this effect even more.

- The questions you used to create your Magickal Life Philosophy can also help you to rediscover the true self that the world has encouraged you to forget.

A question to think about

Now that you know how you like your eggs, what other strong preferences do you have? How comfortable are you in expressing those preferences?

2.3 Stop Apologising for Who You Are

Like becoming full of yourself, the idea of becoming unapologetic can be challenging. It can make you want to put it on the 'to-do someday' list, rather than take steps to embody it now.

In fact, I know that asking you to become both full of yourself *and* unapologetic may seem like too much for one book. That's because these concepts probably go against most of what you've been taught. I'm asking you to tear down and unlearn decades (and decades) of conditioning over several generations.

It's a lot, I know.

It's also incredibly important. So please, bear with me.

First of all, it's important to acknowledge that being unapologetic doesn't mean that you aren't ever sorry. Sometimes an apology is necessary, especially if you've genuinely done something wrong or caused harm.

The problem is that many people – again, especially women – default to apologising in situations where this isn't true. They do it as an automatic reflex whenever they:

- want to de-escalate a situation in which they haven't done anything wrong
- think they might make someone else uncomfortable
- worry that someone else may disagree with their opinion

How often do you apologise?

You might not think that you're a particularly apologetic person. Make a note to watch for apologising in your language over the next few days, though. You may find yourself apologising:

- before asking a question or asking someone to do something for you
- for accidentally standing in front of something that someone else wants to reach for
- for having needs, taking up space or even just existing

You might discover you regularly say, "oops, sorry!" to inanimate objects. Maybe you apologise to door frames or coffee tables if you bump into them. That may seem harmless, perhaps even funny, but it's actually a sign of how deeply conditioned being apologetic has become for us.

You may even find yourself apologising-without-actually-apologising through disempowering language. Perhaps you qualify your requests by adding a word like 'just' to them. You might notice yourself saying, "Can I just ask you to move to the side?" rather than the clearer, "Please could you move to the side."

Another way to apologise-without-apologising is to frequently ask, "Does that make sense?"

It's one thing to genuinely check in with people to ensure they've understood something you've told them. Your tone of voice and purpose in asking can make a huge difference to the effect, though. And when you ask if your opinion makes sense all the time, it can make you sound unsure of both yourself and the opinion.

Society encourages you to be apologetic

In much the same way as you're supposed to be selfless, you're also not supposed to know your worth. You're supposed to be humble. Your value is supposed to only be something that someone else bestows upon you, once you've behaved in the way they expect or approve of.

In fact, you've probably heard the saying 'pride goes before a fall.' So if you *have* had times that you've felt unapologetic and proud of who you are, you've probably been told not to get too cocky or conceited. If you've clearly expressed what's important to you, you've probably met scornful comments about you being too much.

If you've asserted your boundaries and spoken up for your own values and priorities, you've probably met accusations of being too aggressive. If you've moved forward confidently with those values and priorities, you've probably been told you were selfish.

That's a lot of conditioning to overcome.

It may help to realise that these responses almost always come from people who are used to dimming their own light. They've heard these same messages all of their own lives, and are simply passing them on because they've never established their own healthy boundaries.

But reclaiming and embodying your magick means you can't simply accept these messages without question anymore. It means you *must* consciously decide which messages you'll allow to guide your values and priorities, and which you'll refuse to live by any longer.

Don't accept disconnection from your magick as the price of making other people feel better about themselves. Shine brightly – both for yourself, and to remind those people of what's actually possible for them too.

Be like the sun

I'm super pale, so it's only my freckles that give me any sense of colour. I also have quite a bit of red in my hair (at least until it goes fully grey, anyway).

So, with this colouring, you can imagine that the sun and I aren't best friends.

In fact, the sun often just makes me feel hot and bothered.

As I grew up in a seaside fishing village in Cornwall, many of my friends would spend their whole days sunbathing on our local beach. I, on the other hand, just couldn't do that. After anything more than ten minutes, I'd feel too hot and start to burn, even with sunscreen on.

So what did I do?

Did I shout at the sun and try to shame it for being too bright?

Did I tell it to turn its light down because it was making me uncomfortable?

Did I try to throw sea water at it because it burnt my skin?

No, of course not. Those would all be ridiculous!

The sun wasn't doing anything wrong.

It was only being the sun. It was doing exactly what it needed to do to be the sun.

It was up to me to manage how I responded in its presence. So I put on my sunglasses, avoided the midday heat, drank plenty of water and covered up if I had to go outside.

In just the same way, if other people are uncomfortable with your light, it's up to them to manage themselves around you. If you're too bright for them, it's their responsibility to look away. If they're worried about getting 'burnt', they can avoid spending time with you.

It's not your responsibility to shrink or be anything less than your authentic, true self.

Instead, I encourage you to shine brighter. Be more of yourself. Embody the Magick of You fully and completely.

And if you want to help them be less blinded by your brilliance... tell them where they can get some good sunglasses.

It's not about being selfish

Neither being full of yourself nor being unapologetic means you have to become a horrible narcissist who never cares about anyone else. They don't mean that you think you're the ONLY one who deserves to have their needs met either. But you *do* need to become discerning about meeting your own needs, and about how you choose to use your time, energy and resources.

You need to get used to prioritising your own needs over other people's expectations and comfort. Of course, sometimes you'll compromise. Sometimes you *will* put others first, but when you do it, you'll do it consciously. It will be your choice, rather than the default expectation.

As I mentioned previously, when people think of being unapologetic, being full of themselves, or shining brightly, they often think it means being selfish.

They think of toddlers having tantrums and being all 'me, me, me'.

The current self-help industry hasn't helped this concern, as it can make many people very self-focused. It can teach you to believe that life is all about *you*... but that's because the industry itself is still in its infancy. It's still a toddler, and we all know how toddlers can behave.

That's because the self-help field has only been around for a relatively short amount of time. It started coming into its own back in the 1960s and 70s. In the 1960s, the 'flower power' hippy movement introduced people to the idea that they could step away from the establishment and mainstream values. Then, in the 1970s, the rise of professional therapy as we know it today showed people that they had an inner world full of feelings that could be externally validated.

And neither of these developments was inherently bad.

But they're not the full story either.

Of course it can be nice to believe that you're at the centre of the universe, and that everything's about you and your feelings. However, other people are just as important. Their feelings are just as important to them.

The trick is to live your life according to what's true for you, while also letting them live theirs according to what's true for them.

It's about walking the balance between not making other people *more* important than you, but not expecting them to prioritise *your* needs and feelings over their own either.

Your magick matters. And so does the magick of the other eight-ish billion people that you share the planet with.

It's not about toxic positivity either

In recent years, we've seen a huge growth in good-vibes-only philosophies, insta-therapy and shelf-help (self-help books that stay on your shelf). Some of this can be useful to make us feel a little better in the short term, but it doesn't bring about any real change or transformation.

And sometimes, it can be actively toxic. For example, insisting on good vibes only dismisses the very real experiences of the beautiful but brutal world we live in.

Meanwhile, insta-therapy can be great to make you question something or quickly validate an experience. What it doesn't do is address the situation, habits and behaviours that you need to focus on to bring about long-term, sustainable change.

And those self-help books on your shelf can convince you that you're making progress and doing the work. But if all you're doing is simply collecting them, or quickly reading each one and then moving on to the next, nothing will change. You need to actually try implementing the ideas in those books (yes, including this one), which takes time and effort.

We need to move from the idea of self-help or even of simply helping ourselves, to the idea of maturing into growth and development.

This is the energy of being unapologetic.

Being unapologetic is about maturing yourself, not infantilising yourself.

It's about recognising what you need and having clear boundaries around what you'll accept. That means it's also about:

- seeing the bigger picture, where you fit into it and how you can contribute
- holding a higher vision for both yourself and the world around you
- refusing to default to the easy option, and instead insisting on the one that brings growth for yourself and those around you

Being unapologetic is about recognising your own magick, and realising that it's no better (or worse) than anyone else's magick. At the same time, it's about knowing that the richest experience of life happens when everyone connects with and embodies their own magick. It's also about accepting that this rich experience will be far more fulfilling than the bland, fake, homogenised version of life that our society sells us.

Being unapologetic also means giving yourself the time and space to consider and make conscious choices that draw on both your intellect and your intuition. It's about refusing to feel rushed or pressured simply because someone else expects or wants something from you now.

It's about choosing what's best for you in the long term, not just the easy, quick fix in the moment.

It's about knowing yourself and how you best contribute to the world – knowing that everything is both all about you and not at all about you.

It's about being able to make calm, clear decisions that support you and the person you're becoming. It's about contributing to creating the world that you want to live in around you.

And it's about naming and claiming who you are and what's important to you.

Activity: **What's in a name?**

Who you think you are and what you call yourself matters. Words are important.

In fact, as we said back in *Chapter 1.1 – What is Magick?*, words are magickal. They're tools that we use to cast our spells into the world, which then create and shape our reality.

Words enchant us or curse us. They can lift us up, motivate us or have us doubting ourselves.

Words bring our thoughts into reality.

There's an old adage: sticks and stones may break my bones, but words will never hurt me. I don't think that's quite true. Broken bones may heal, but some words are never forgotten.

This means how you talk to yourself is crucial. It also means that what you call yourself and how you speak to yourself are fundamental in how you view yourself.

How do you describe yourself?

What language do you use when you're describing yourself to yourself?

Complete the sentence:

"I am..."

The two little words 'I am' may seem small, but whatever you put after them can change everything.

Read each of the following 'I am' statements silently to yourself. Notice how you feel, what sensations you experience and what thoughts and memories come to mind for each one:

- I am gifted
- I am loved
- I am magickal
- I am passionate
- I am powerful
- I am resourceful
- I am unapologetic

Two little words, three letters, can start to change how you see yourself. Next, try saying each of them out loud:

- I am gifted
- I am loved
- I am magickal
- I am passionate
- I am powerful
- I am resourceful
- I am unapologetic

Choose your words carefully

You get to define yourself, so choose the words you use consciously and carefully.

You might still not feel gifted, loved, magickal, passionate, powerful, resourceful or unapologetic. But how might that change if you add the three little letters y.e.t. to the end of that sentence?

Try it. Add them on.

Say, "I might not feel gifted, loved, magickal, passionate, powerful, resourceful or unapologetic... yet."

With that one little word, even if you don't feel it right now, the feeling becomes available to you.

Remember that owning your magick doesn't have to be about big changes. Often, little switches (like simply adding on a 'yet') can make a big difference.

That one word, those three letters, can step you out of the energy of overwhelm and stuckness, and into the energy of possibility.

Perhaps you're not feeling fully connected to your own magick *yet*, but you want to be.

So, ask yourself, who do you need to become to reconnect with your Magickal Life Philosophy and embody it at all times?

Claiming your magickal moniker

We said in the activity above that how you describe yourself matters. And what you *call* yourself matters even more.

The name you give yourself connects you to your identity and individuality.

Calling yourself 'a hopeless case', 'a screwup' or even a 'muggle', will start you believing – and then reinforce the belief – that you're hopeless, not enough or unmagickal.

If, however, you call yourself something that aligns with your Magickal Life Philosophy, you'll reinforce the very Magick of You.

Anna Bellissima, ceremonial magician and copywriter, once wrote in an email that creating a magickal moniker gives you permission to do, be and have whatever you want.

I loved that. It really resonated with me.

It reminded me of why I claimed the word 'Witch'. So now, if someone says, "Rebecca you can't do that!" my response is, "Of course I can! I'm a Witch!" <insert magickal cackle>

What magickal moniker could you claim for yourself that would give you permission to live your Magickal Life Philosophy and say yes to yourself, your desires and magick? Perhaps it might be:

- Ethereal Enchantress
- Fun-loving Fairy
- Magnificent Mage
- Magickal Maven
- Modern-day Witch
- Powerful Magician
- Sensual Sorceress
- Shining Star
- Wild Wizard

Claiming one of these titles could feel intimidating. They might seem easy to dismiss as silly, as all of your old conditioning and judgements come up.

After all, who are you to claim such a bold title?

Or perhaps you associate these names with something less than empowering. As an example, let's look at 'Witch'. There's no question that it's an emotive word.

For many people, it conjures up archetypal, fairy tale images of an evil old woman who causes trouble and uses her magick to harm others. Many women were (and are still) called witches because they spoke up against expectations and societal norms. They were labelled as 'too much' and persecuted.

That accusation of being too much is still used to keep us silent – silent about injustices, silent about our own needs and silent in our own choices. Perhaps that's why witches can also symbolise all that's wild, powerful and unapologetic.

This symbolism can scare many people, including other women who want to be all of those things.

That's exactly why the word 'Witch' is important to me.

Which name helps you reclaim your magick?

For me, the word 'Witch' is less about old stereotypes, and more about remembering and reclaiming the truth of who you are.

When you reclaim this truth, you get to celebrate your wild edges, and reclaim your inner power, as we talked about earlier.

This often means breaking down old belief paradigms. It means working outside of all that you've been taught about what's right and wrong, good and bad, expected and acceptable.

And yes, it will mean that some people may label you as 'too much'.

But when you honour yourself, your energy and what's important to you, other people's opinions don't stop you from doing what you know you need to do.

I hope that by the end of this book, you'll be more full of yourself and unapologetic than you were at the start. Because when you are, you can stand tall and firm as you celebrate ALL of yourself and embody both your magick and your Magickal Life Philosophy.

Key insights to take with you

- Our society encourages us to constantly apologise for being ourselves and taking up space in the world.

- There's nothing wrong with apologising if you've actually caused someone else harm, but over-apologising can disconnect you from your worth.

- Being unapologetic isn't being selfish or embracing toxic positivity – it's about recognising that you need to embody your own magick and everyone else needs to embody theirs.

- Reconnecting with your magick starts with looking at how you describe yourself to yourself, and the name you call yourself.

A question to think about

How would you most love to describe your authentic self to yourself? What would need to change in your life for that to become your reality?

2.4 Using Your Magickal Life Philosophy

How to experience more of your Magickal Life Philosophy

Knowing what you want to experience more of in your life is the first step to experiencing it... but it's *only* the first step.

Taking action to bring more of those feelings into your life is just as important. And unless you take action based on it, your Magickal Life Philosophy will never be more than a fun exercise you tried when you worked through this book.

So, once you've spent some time imagining a life filled with the feelings and values you want, don't stop there. Keep going by identifying a single word that sums up the feelings.

Perhaps your word sums up all the feelings you want to experience – something like 'compassion' or 'presence' or 'joy'.

Or maybe it describes how you feel when you're experiencing them – perhaps 'expansive' or 'light' or 'bold'.

When I've done this exercise with others, they've come up with words like 'luxurious', 'bold', 'golden', 'luminous', 'unstoppable' or even our friend from the last chapter, 'unapologetic'.

The only rule is that your word must be positive and affirming.

For example, a phrase like 'not afraid' is a good start. Knowing what you *don't* want can be an important step to identifying what you do. But what are the positive aspects of not being afraid? What does not being afraid allow you to do or become? Perhaps it might be 'courageous' or 'bold' or 'free'.

Whatever your one word is, take it and start to use it as the guiding essence of living into your Magickal Life Philosophy.

Each day ask yourself, "What can I do to experience more of *this word* in my life?"

Use the word as a filter to run your decisions through. Whenever you have a choice to make, ask yourself, "Which decision aligns me most with my word?"

A little is better than none

Of course, some choices will feel impossible to bring your Magickal Life Philosophy into. If this happens, it's OK. The important thing is that you considered your philosophy before choosing.

Other times, you might not be able to make a choice that's completely aligned with your philosophy. You might still be able to bring a little of it in, though, or use it to amend the options that are available to you a little.

For example, let's say that your word was 'expansive', and you needed to make a quick decision between two difficult choices. Neither decision option would be likely to make you feel expansive... but nor would staying permanently stuck in the energy of procrastination and indecisiveness.

So in this case, you could ask for a little more time to make the decision, even if it was just an hour.

You still may not like either of the options available to you, but at least you've taken the time to check in with yourself. You've run the decision through the lens of your 'expansive' Magickal Life Philosophy. And you've done your best to bring the energy of expansiveness into your choice.

You can use this process for anything, and each time you do, it connects you with a little more of your own magick. It quietens down the expectations and 'should' energy from the world around you, allowing you to reconnect with what's really important to you.

Get creative and have fun with it.

As you go through your day, get curious about how you could bring a little more of your Magickal Life Philosophy into your everyday life.

To start with, this may feel clunky. But it will very quickly become your new normal, and you'll enjoy feeling more connected, fulfilled and on-purpose in all areas of your life.

Just like when you were doing those squats, the more you practise, the easier the process will become.

Embodying your life philosophy with magickal knickers

One of my favourite ways to really embed your Magickal Life Philosophy into each and every day is to choose what I call magickal knickers. Yes, the magickal knickers from the Introduction!

Here's how it works. Every morning, when you begin to get dressed, try choosing knickers that reflect how you want to feel that day.

Which pair will make you feel most aligned with your Magickal Life Philosophy? This could be about their size, material, colour, memories or just how you feel wearing them.

Perhaps you want more energy for the day, so you pick a red pair of knickers.

Perhaps you want to feel more supported, so you choose a pair that holds you in.

Perhaps you want to experience pure freedom, so you choose to wear none at all.

It's completely up to you what knickers you choose to wear. It doesn't matter if there's a dress code or uniform at work. In most cases, your underwear choices are 100% your own.

Doing this means that, each day when you choose your magickal knickers, you take a moment to pause and connect with what's important to you. You prioritise yourself and your needs.

You start each day by putting yourself first.

This then makes it easier to build on these positive choices throughout your day. Plus, each time during the day that you see or become aware of your knickers, it's a quick little reminder of your Magickal Life Philosophy.

Empty out your knicker drawer and look at each pair of knickers in there individually.

Ask yourself what feelings that pair evokes in you.

Does it reflect your truth?

Does it reflect how you feel about yourself?

What do your knickers say about you?

Which knickers could represent different aspects of your Magickal Life Philosophy?

Do you need to get rid of any, or purchase some new ones that better reflect what you want from your life?

How could you change your knickers to help you connect more deeply with your Magickal Life Philosophy?

Start consciously wearing your knickers

Once you've identified a few pairs of knickers that reflect what you want to experience in life, actually start choosing to wear them

Try consciously choosing your knickers each day for the next week.

Notice how you feel at different points in the day when you wear knickers that align with how you want to experience the world.

Finally, at the end of the week, reflect on how you've shown up in your life. Have you felt more connected, present and magickal?

Have you become more aware of living your Magickal Life Philosophy?

Expand this conscious choosing out to the rest of your day

Of course, knickers aren't the only thing you can consciously choose. Once you've chosen which knickers you'll wear, you could also then choose a body wash, shampoo or lotion that reflected your Magickal Life Philosophy.

Then you might start to choose a breakfast that aligns with your philosophy – whether that's the food you eat, the environment you eat it in or the people you eat it with.

There are hundreds of ways you can start to add your Magickal Life Philosophy word into your day. Don't let it be complicated or a chore. Just have fun and actually begin.

After a few weeks of using your word, you may want to check in with yourself. Make sure it's still the right word for you. And if it's anything less than perfect, remember that you can change it.

You might discover that, when you first did this exercise, you'd got caught up in trying to choose a 'good' feeling or value for your word. You might realise that the value you chose was one you felt you should pick because that's what a 'good' person would choose.

But your Magickal Life Philosophy needs to be all about you and what you truly want for your life. It can only help to reconnect you with your magick if it's free of other people's judgements, expectations and opinions.

Identify three to five activities that you do routinely each morning. These might include:

- having a shower
- making a hot drink
- eating your breakfast
- reading or listening to music
- meditating
- exercising
- making your bed
- driving to work

Start to think about how you could bring more of your Magickal Life Philosophy into each of your activities. For example, if your Magickal Life Philosophy word was 'nourished', you might bring more nourishment into your morning activities by:

- choosing a soap or shower gel that leaves your skin feeling nourished, and applying a rich, nourishing cream to your face and body afterwards
- trying out different morning drinks to find one that feels more nourishing if you realise your usual coffee is leaving you jittery
- trying out different breakfast foods, or eating in a different space, to see what feels most nourishing, and giving thanks before you eat to bring in additional nourishment energy

- choosing books or music that nourish your soul or intellect
- playing with different styles of meditation until you find one or two that feel truly nourishing
- choosing a form of exercise you really enjoy and celebrating the way it nourishes your body and mind
- giving thanks for the nourishing rest you had the night before, or that you'll have in the coming evening, when you get back under the covers
- leaving yourself extra time to get to your destination, playing your favourite music or using your favourite fragrance to nourish your senses while you drive

Once again, there's no absolute right or wrong to your choices. One person might find that swapping their morning jog for some gentle stretching feels more nourishing. For another, getting their blood pumping and endorphins flowing would be the more nourishing choice. A third person might find exercising in the afternoon was actually far more nourishing for them than doing anything in the morning.

Keep experimenting with different parts of your morning routine and discover which activities best connect you to your Magickal Life Philosophy.

If you start doubting

If you find yourself doubting your Magickal Life Philosophy, it's time to explore how much other people's 'junk' values and philosophies (see *Chapter 2.1 – Understanding Your Magickal Life Philosophy*) might be influencing you.

Start by asking yourself:

- Where do you try to measure up to other people's ideas of success?
- In what areas of your life does our social-media-influencer culture have you comparing yourself to someone else's ideals?
- Where do you silence yourself for fear of not fitting in or getting it wrong?
- In what areas of your life do you doubt yourself and give your power away by seeking external validation?

If your answers show that you're letting other people's values and opinions sneak in, it's time to reduce the junk in your life philosophy. It's time to bring in more of your own magick.

Remember that your Magickal Life Philosophy won't ever be a finished product. As you grow and discover more about yourself, it will continue to grow with you. That means you'll need to constantly refine it to suit you and your needs as they are at the time.

Also, I don't want you to limit yourself to striving for love and light or grace and ease in your Magickal Life Philosophy.

Much like the good-vibes-only philosophies we talked about in the last chapter, these may sound great. The problem is that they often overlook the importance of taking responsibility for yourself, your actions and your behaviours. That's because they focus on the outcomes being light and easy, when the reality of the world and life – much like the reality of you and your magick – is much more complex.

How will you act on your Magickal Life Philosophy?

The rules you set for your life (AKA your Magickal Life Philosophy) weave together your intentions and values into practical action that helps you to live intentionally and fulfil your desires.

As we said at the beginning of this chapter, simply having a Magickal Life Philosophy won't change your life. Taking actions that are informed by, and that align with, your philosophy will.

Choosing to live your Magickal Life Philosophy informs your choices, which in turn influences your behaviours and impacts your experience of the world.

There's much in the world that's completely out of your control. So make sure that you focus your attention, energy and power on what you *can* control. What choices can you make? What actions can you take? What practical things can you do that will start to make some of the impact you desire on your life?

And if you need support in actually *doing* what you know you need to do, the next section – which covers cultivating a magickal mindset – offers several helpful tools.

Key insights to take with you

- While selecting a Magickal Life Philosophy is important, it's only the first step: you need to start acting on it too.

- You might not be able to infuse every decision you make with your Magickal Life Philosophy, but even just bringing some of it in is often better than nothing.

- You can bring your Magickal Life Philosophy into your daily routines like showering, eating breakfast or exercising too.

- If you start doubting your philosophy, examine it closely to see whether other people's 'junk' values, opinions and priorities have crept into it.

A question to think about

What would be the most possible fun you could imagine having with bringing your Magickal Life Philosophy into your daily life?

Section 3: **Your Magickal Mindset**

Creating the Magickal MIND mindset that aligns you with
the results you want to manifest

3.1 Cultivating a Magickal Mindset

Living your Magickal Life Philosophy requires the right mindset

Creating change, manifesting your desires or staying on track with your habits to support those desires all require a specific kind of mindset. I call this mindset 'the Magickal MIND'. And remember when I said I loved acronyms? Well, in this section, we'll explore exactly what each of the letters in the word 'MIND' stands for.

A Magickal MIND mindset helps you to take the actions you know you need to take to live according to your Magickal Life Philosophy. More than this, it helps you to *keep* taking those actions... and stops you from holding yourself back or sabotaging yourself. So without this mindset, you probably won't get the results you want, or at least not consistently.

Here's why. Think back to a time when you tried to create change in the past, implement a new routine or manifest your desires. Perhaps you might have been successful when you did this... for a while.

Still, at some point along the way, you probably felt as though you'd done everything you needed to do, but still weren't getting the results you wanted. No doubt you quickly began to feel disheartened and unable to understand why your desires just weren't manifesting.

Eventually, you just gave up.

This is where cultivating a Magickal MIND mindset would have helped.

Without a Magickal MIND, you end up working against yourself

Maintaining a Magickal MIND mindset isn't about constantly being positive or having to stay 'high-vibe'. I've already talked about the dangers of toxic positivity in *Chapter 2.3 – Stop Apologising for Who You Are*. So I'm certainly not recommending bringing this into your mindset.

Instead, a Magickal MIND is about conscious creation. It's about aligning with your magick while being 100% authentic to you and your circumstances. And without this mindset, you can't align yourself with the change you desire.

That's because you can do all of the things that you think you need to do on a practical level. But if your mind and subconscious beliefs aren't aligned with the result you want, they'll pull you back and keep you from achieving it.

They'll encourage you to doubt yourself.

They'll tell you that you're not good enough, or that you don't deserve whatever it is that you want to achieve.

They'll tell you that it's too hard to create what you desire.

Sure enough, with those voices undermining the work you're doing, it becomes really difficult to get where you want to go. Keeping the momentum going becomes too hard.

This is particularly true if the changes you want to make are ones that other people around you don't understand or agree with. In these cases, the messages you pick up on – or perhaps even overtly hear – from these people combine with the messages from your own mind and subconscious beliefs.

And the resulting combination is often just too overwhelming.

Reclaiming the Magick of You requires more than just wishful thinking or hoping that something will go your way.

It's not enough to continuously plan either.

Nor is it enough to simply try to visualise your desires into reality.

It's not even enough to force yourself to do all the practical things that you think you should be doing.

Instead, reclaiming the Magick of You requires knowing that you can consciously direct your thoughts, intentions, actions and energy to align with and support the life you want.

So when you really want to reconnect with your magick, cultivating a Magickal MIND mindset is one of the most important factors in your success.

Activity: Exploring your history with manifesting and mindset

Think about two times in the past when you've tried to deliberately manifest a desire, achieve a goal or just create a specific outcome:

- one time when what you wanted ended up happening
- one time when it didn't

Once you've identified these two times, take out your journal (or equivalent), and write your answers to the following questions.

For the successful time...

- How long did it take before your desire showed up?
- How long did the desire continue to be important in your life after it showed up?
- Did achieving it feel the way you'd hoped it would?
- Is the desire still relevant in your life today?
- What new possibility or path did achieving it lead you to follow next?

For the unsuccessful time...

- How long did you keep working towards your desire?
- When and why did you stop working towards it?
- How did you feel about not achieving your desire at the time?
- How might your life have changed – both for the better and for the worse – if you *had* achieved it?

- Would you have been ready and had enough support available for that change at the time?
- What new possibility or path did *not* achieving your desire create in your life?

Then, notice what worked for you and what didn't. What potential outcomes, circumstances or activities motivated you to keep going and overcome any obstacles? Which of them led to you being unsuccessful?

As you get ready to explore the Magickal MIND process, it can be useful to identify which of the areas you've already experienced success with, and where you may need some additional support.

Understanding the Magickal MIND elements

The Magickal MIND process is a step-by-step system to keep yourself aligned with what's truly important to you. It helps to give you the inspiration and momentum you need to keep going when things get difficult. It also provides a foundation that you can return to time and time again to help you navigate any challenges that you come up against.

To support you in creating and maintaining your Magickal MIND mindset, I've created four steps for you to follow and check in with. Following them will help you to stay truly aligned with the desires you're working towards. And if you find yourself getting knocked off course, these steps will help to nudge you back in the right direction.

The four steps that make up the MIND acronym are:

- **M – Motivated mind**: first, check that you have the correct motivations for your desire. If you don't, you're simply wasting your time, energy and resources.

- **I – Intentional mind**: next, ensure that you're staying on track with your intended desire, and not getting distracted by things that don't matter.

- **N – Nourished mind**: remind yourself that you have support in manifesting your desire, and lean into that support instead of doing everything on your own.

- **D – Dedicated mind**: finally, check that you're ready and willing to do what it takes to get where you want to go, and recommit to the result you want.

When all of these pieces are in place, bringing your intentions and desires into reality becomes so much easier. There's no more guesswork or hoping, and no more fighting against yourself to keep moving forward.

There's just a step-by-step system for you to follow to create a Magickal MIND mindset.

And in the remainder of this section, I'll take you through each of the steps in detail.

------ /// ------

Key insights to take with you

- Living your Magickal Life Philosophy requires you to take constant action, but action on its own often isn't enough.

- That's because even if you do everything you need to do on a practical level, if your mind and beliefs aren't aligned, it can all become too hard.

- This is especially true when you want to make changes that other people in your life don't understand or agree with.

- A Magickal MIND mindset keeps your mind Motivated for the right reasons, Intentional and focused, Nourished with the right support and Dedicated to your desire.

A question to think about

How does your current mindset support you in achieving your desires? How does it undermine you?

The Motivated MIND Mindset

Motivation is personal

When you set your intentions, it's essential to get clear on what's motivating your desire.

It's easy to find yourself setting goals or focusing on desires based on what other people think you should want. But you have to want your intention for yourself.

You're also going to need to put time, effort and energy into bringing this desire into reality. That means you have to really *want* it, not just feel like it's something that'd be nice to have.

I've worked with many people who've achieved big things in their lives simply because it was expected of them. Perhaps they went to university, trained for a particular career or married a certain type of person.

They might have achieved these things because they felt pressure to conform with what their family desired for them. Or perhaps they wanted to fit in with what their religion or culture expected of them or what society demanded of them.

The problem was that when they walked the path that had been laid out for them, achieving their goal didn't bring them any joy. Instead, they ended up feeling dissatisfied and frustrated.

That doesn't mean their life up to that point was bad. It just wasn't completely theirs, and they never had the chance to explore what they genuinely wanted for themselves. They didn't get to express themselves fully.

If you're like many of these people, you'll recognise the sense of holding conflicting motivations around the outcomes you're working towards. On the one hand, you want to fit in and not upset those you care about. On the other, you want to step away from everyone else's expectations and follow the path that's authentic for you.

This conflict can leave you exhausted as you constantly take three steps towards the life you desire, and then other people's judgements and expectations pull you two steps back. That 'push-pull' energy doesn't align you with achieving your desired outcome either.

This is why you need to be clear on the motivation behind your intentions and desires. To start with, for each desire, I suggest asking yourself:

- Why is this intention important to you?
- How will your life be different when you've achieved it?
- Why do you want the change it will bring to your life?
- What's the outcome that you want to achieve?
- How does your life, and the lives of those around you, look and feel after you've achieved the desire or worked towards it?
- Is this something that you truly want? Or is it something that you think you *should* do or attain?
- Does your desired outcome align with your values and your Magickal Life Philosophy?

Take some time to start getting clear on the motivations behind your intention.

Why do you REALLY want to do the thing?

A quick way to check the motivation behind your choices is to simply ask yourself, "Why is this important to me?"

Then, when you have your answer, ask again, "And why is that important to me?"

Finally, when you have that answer, ask yourself one more time, "And why is *that* important to me?"

For example, people will often tell me that they want to manifest X amount of money.

When I first ask them why they want that money, some of them say it's about meeting their fundamental needs. Perhaps they want to have enough money for unexpected expenses such as medical bills, house maintenance or car repairs - or just to afford nutritious food for their kids.

Meanwhile, other people will list the material things that they want to purchase with more money or the debts they want to pay off.

When I ask them the second why, though, their answers start to get more thoughtful. The first group might say that they grew up poor and don't want their children to struggle the way they did. Or maybe they saw what happened when someone they loved had an emergency medical situation and couldn't afford to get the care they needed.

Meanwhile, the second group might talk about how much more comfortable their lives would be if they had the latest gadget or car. Or perhaps they'd tell me how much more they'd enjoy life if they could move into a bigger house or travel business class.

By the time we get to the third why, the answers get even more thoughtful. The first group might realise that what they truly want is safety and security for themselves and their families. That's an intrinsic motivator that's likely to be strong enough to align them with the outcome they want. The money is important, but it's not actually their main motivation. There may also be other ways that they can create that safety and security for themselves.

The second group might realise that they'd felt they needed more money to fit in with other people. Or perhaps they might realise they were trying to live a lifestyle that someone else had told them they should want, or that was what they thought a 'successful' person would do and have.

Maybe they realise that they wanted money to enjoy the freedom of choice that having more than you need to simply survive can bring. But perhaps they can find that freedom in other ways that don't rely on having more money – sometimes ways that feel more aligned to who they are.

Understanding your motivation is essential because even people with seemingly similar intentions and desires will have very different journeys to achieve them. Each person has different obstacles to navigate, requiring different skills and attributes from them.

It's also important because there's no 'one size fits all' for motivation. Nor are there any shortcuts. There's only knowing yourself and being honest about your motivations. And when you do this, you can start making choices and taking actions that align with your magick, instead of choosing from a place of 'should'.

Activity: **Your motivational why**

Take a moment to write out an intention you have or an outcome you want to achieve.

Ask yourself how much the outcome excites you on a scale of 1-10 where:

- 1 means 'It'd be nice...'
- 10 means 'Woo hoo, yes! This is incredible and would completely fulfil me!'

Then ask yourself *why* this is important to you.

When you get your answer to that first why, ask why that answer is important to you.

Finally, ask why that second answer is important to you.

Take the time to be honest with yourself as you uncover the real motivation behind your intention. Remember: you're ensuring that this is indeed your own motivation, and not a fear or an expectation in disguise.

When you've established your true motivation, ask yourself, "How does me having this impact the people around me?"

It's important to acknowledge how having something will affect those around you because it reminds you that we're all connected. This keeps you full of yourself and your dreams and desires, while ensuring that you don't become overly self-obsessed. It reminds you that you're responsible both for yourself and for the world you live in.

If the thing you want will have a positive impact on others, knowing this can help to motivate you and encourage you to pursue it.

If the impact will genuinely be negative (which is very rare), knowing this allows you to refine your desired outcome to avoid potentially harming those around you. However, bear in mind that actually harming other people is very different to making them uncomfortable with you changing.

Understanding your motivations makes the process smoother

When you're aligned with where you're going and motivated to get there, it's a bit like slipstreaming through the water in a canoe. You paddle a little to stay on course, but most of your movement comes from aligning with the flowing river.

Maybe you're aware of the odd, gentle wave, but you're confident in yourself and your skills, so that's OK. You see the wave. You're not afraid of it. You're motivated, so you just keep going. You may even enjoy playing in the waves, honing your skills and recognising the improvement and progress you're making.

However, sometimes, even though you're determined to achieve something, your motivation for achieving it isn't aligned with your true desire. Deep down, you know this intention isn't for you, but you ignore that inner knowing, for a while at least.

When you do the 'why' exercise above, you might realise that you only want this outcome because you feel like you owe it to your family. Or perhaps it seems easier to strive for the outcome than explain to other people why you don't want to work towards it.

In our canoeing analogy, you're still paddling... but this time you're dragging lots of unnecessary weight behind your canoe. The weight is made of expectations, judgements and shame, and you're trying to paddle whilst dragging it behind you. Maybe you're dragging a large buoy that's attached with tangles of weed-covered rope. Perhaps it even feels like you're dragging an entire second canoe that's floating side-on to yours, and some of it is hidden under the water.

So you're paddling and battling to move through the water. You're still moving, but it's really, really hard. Plus, because you're so focused on moving forward at all costs, and some of what you're dragging behind you is underwater, you can't see everything that's there.

And the more you struggle forward, the more stuff gets tangled up in the mess that's dragging behind you.

Taking the time to understand your motivation helps you to realise just how much extra weight you're carrying. When you're aware of it, you can cut it free, releasing you to go on your way with greater ease.

It also ensures you'll enjoy your achievements

Sometimes, the surface motivation you feel to manifest something that's not aligned is strong enough to overcome the 'drag'. So you get to your destination, but when you do, you feel exhausted. The achievement doesn't feel as good as you expected it to.

Instead of feeling fulfilled and proud of yourself for what you've achieved, you just feel flat.

As an example, one woman came to work with me when she realised that something wasn't right in her life. She'd worked really hard to get the car of her dreams in the exact colour that she wanted. She'd thought that once she had this car, she'd feel the way she wanted to: successful, fulfilled and finally good enough.

So she bought it, and although it was perfect, everything else in her life and how she felt about it stayed exactly the same. Nothing changed, except that she now had a different car.

Not only did she still have all the feelings of not being successful or good enough, but now she was hugely disappointed in her car too.

She'd met the external measures of success she'd been trying to live up to.... but she hadn't allowed herself to connect with what she'd really wanted underneath the surface desire.

That's why, when you're looking at your motivations, you have to make sure that they're what you truly want. Not only will getting clear on this ensure that you know how to navigate the obstacles – the waves – that you come across. It will also ensure that the time, effort and energy you put into overcoming them are worth it.

Difficult doesn't mean wrong

Unless you're extremely, unusually lucky, obstacles *will* come up as you're working towards manifesting your desires. And unless you're resolute in your motivation, when those obstacles come up, you'll find yourself just giving up. You won't have the energy to work out how to overcome each obstacle.

Often, people see obstacles as The Universe telling them they're not meant to have their desire. They believe that if the life they wanted was supposed to happen, it would be easy.

I believe that obstacles exist to give us the opportunity to check in with ourselves about how motivated we are to make our desires come true.

Imagine hearing about the stunning views you could see at the top of a mountain. You decide to walk up the mountain to experience them for yourself... but on your way up the path, you come across a boulder.

In that moment, you have a decision to make.

You could decide to turn back because you're sure that the boulder is there for a reason. Perhaps you're just not supposed to see the view today (or any day until someone else clears the boulder away).

But that's not the only interpretation you could have for the boulder. Maybe it's there to encourage you to take a different, better path to the summit that you weren't yet aware of.

Or it could be there because working out how to navigate around the boulder will make you stronger. Perhaps the additional strength you develop whilst navigating it could be what you need to get to your destination and enjoy the view as well.

When I was in my early 20s, I walked the Coast to Coast of England, which involves walking from one side of the country to the other. At that time in my life, I hadn't done much long-distance walking.

The traditional route went from the West Coast to the East Coast. When I looked at the map, however, I realised that this meant starting in the steepest terrain of the Lake District and ending with the flatter moorlands.

So I decided to walk it in reverse, from east to west. That way, I could get fitter in the first part of the walk before I had to hike the steeper terrain.

This was a terrible idea for many reasons, one being that the weather was in my face the whole time. There was so much wind and rain. Still though, by the time I got to the end of the walk, I certainly felt fit enough for the mountains. So while the wind and rain were definitely obstacles, overcoming them helped me to build the fitness I needed to complete the walk.

Getting clear on your motivations for your desires and why they're important to you also helps you to navigate the obstacles you encounter. It helps you to understand whether each obstacle is telling you to turn back, go in a different direction or keep going and develop what you need along the way.

As another example, you might not like the idea of studying for eight years to finally have the career you want. But if you really want that career, you'll find the motivation to show up and do the work – even when not doing so may be the easier choice.

Similarly, declining a night out so that you can prepare for a presentation or interview the next day may not be the easy (or fun) choice. Your friends may get annoyed at you, and you may even prefer to go out with friends than prepare. When you're motivated enough to advance your career, though, making the hard choice enables you to show up much more prepared. It also helps you to make the most of the opportunities that move you towards the life you desire.

Beyond this, focusing on your authentic why gives you the motivation to stretch outside of your comfort zone. You may not like the stretch, but you understand why it's necessary, and you're prepared to embrace the growth.

Whereas if you're doing something out of expectation, conditioning or because you feel you should, coming up against an obstacle will usually make you turn back. Or, even worse, it might just leave you standing and looking at the obstacle. You might put your life in a holding position, and end up feeling stuck, frustrated and dissatisfied.

That kind of life might not be terrible, but it certainly won't be magickal.

Obstacles can tell you when you don't want something enough

While obstacles don't automatically mean a path is wrong for you, sometimes that realisation is a gift they provide.

That's because if you're fully motivated and committed, you become resourceful and curious about how to best overcome tough obstacles. You may reach out and enlist the help, knowledge and expertise of others. You might give yourself time to learn new skills to overcome the obstacles.

As a result, you *do* overcome them, or at least you give it your best go. And perhaps you find a different, better way forward.

Other times, though, you discover when you hit an obstacle that you just aren't motivated enough to work out how to overcome it. Maybe your desire genuinely isn't that important to you right now. Or perhaps you don't have the time, energy or resources to give it the attention that it needs at the moment.

Both realisations are great.

Being truly motivated means you can keep working towards your desire with clarity and confidence that you're on the right path.

Knowing that you're not motivated enough is also great because it gives you permission to stop trying to force yourself to achieve something you don't really want or can't fully commit to at this time. Instead, you can free up that time and energy to discover what you genuinely want and can actually work towards.

Asking yourself why isn't a one-time thing when it comes to reconnecting with your magick.

Having a Motivated MIND mindset means that every time you encounter an obstacle, you take a moment to check in with yourself and ask three questions:

1. **Are you still on the right path?**

   Is this desire something you still want for yourself?

   Does it move you towards the future you want to create?

2. **Are you still willing to do what it takes to make it happen?**

   Are you willing to put the time, energy and resources into not only pursuing this goal, but also prioritising it?

3. **Are you willing and able to do what it takes to overcome this obstacle?**

   Do you want to become resilient enough to overcome it?

   Are you willing to ask for the help and support you need?

   Are you ready to embrace the growth required to overcome the challenges?

Maybe the answer to each of these questions is yes. If so, brilliant. Keep going.

But if the answer is no, that's brilliant too. Now you can give yourself permission to let this desire go and focus on discovering what you *actually* want instead.

Staying motivated

Just like asking yourself why, getting motivated isn't a one-time thing. Your motivation is something you need to check in with time and time again.

Some days, you won't feel ready to create the change you desire. You won't feel courageous enough or confident enough. You certainly won't feel ready.

That's OK. At this point, you just need to take action, no matter how small. You won't always wake up *feeling* motivated, but you can create an action plan that keeps you connected with your motivation.

Ask yourself what actions you can do to keep that connection strong.

The more you do something, the easier it becomes. If you create a habit (more about habits in *Section 4: Magickal Habits*) of taking action to connect with your motivation, getting and staying motivated will become easier.

Habits that connect you to your motivation could include:

- creating a vision board based on the feelings and emotions that your outcome will bring

- repeating affirmations throughout the day to remind you of your why (see *Chapter 4.3 – Soul Vitamin Habits* for some ideas)

- spending at least five minutes each day visualising your success

- creating a playlist of your favourite music that inspires and motivates you

- moving your body in a way that energises you

- listing all of the ways that your skills and personal attributes help you achieve things and overcome obstacles, and how they've done this in the past

Key insights to take with you

- Motivation is personal, and if it's not intrinsic to you and your authentic desires, it won't help you to align with achieving them.

- It's also often complex and layered, so you'll sometimes need to dig beneath your initial why to uncover your real motivation for an intention.

- Understanding your true motivations can make the process of achieving your desires smoother, and give you more resilience when you encounter obstacles on your path.

- Coming across an obstacle doesn't necessarily mean you're on the wrong path, but it can help you to realise when you're not motivated enough for a given desire.

- Staying motivated requires checking in with yourself every time you encounter an obstacle to ensure you're still on the right path.

A question to think about

When has the motivation to overcome an obstacle
helped you to develop the strength or skills you
needed to enjoy manifesting a desire more? When has
it helped you to find a better path?

3.3 The Intentional MIND Mindset

Without intention, motivation is just a feeling

You now know that your desire is aligned with what you really want, and that it's free of other people's judgements and expectations. You're confident in what you've chosen to manifest and motivated to make it happen. Now it's time to back up all that motivation by taking intentional action to move you in the right direction.

Your motivation created the momentum to start bringing your desired change into reality. Now, taking intentional actions keeps you on track with moving towards that desire.

Becoming intentional with your thoughts, energy, resources and choices ensures that any action you take in your daily life supports your progress towards your desired outcome. It also increases your confidence in focusing your attention on what matters most to you.

That's because when you're intentional, you make powerful choices that support your desires. This can mean choosing to take an action. But it can also mean choosing to *stop* doing something that you know doesn't work for you or that has held you back in the past.

Either way, you consciously choose what's important to you, again and again and again.

You choose yourself.

You choose your energy.

You choose the Magick of You.

It's no good *knowing* what you want and then doing nothing to manifest it.

Too often, people think working with their magick to manifest their desires means making a decision and then sitting back and waiting for The Universe to make it happen. All the visioning, affirmations or positive thinking in the world won't bring your desire into reality unless you also take action.

Well... occasionally this can work, but the times are few and far between.

For the most part, real magick happens when desire meets aligned, intentional action.

Creating the right conditions for your desire

When you're clear on what you want, making it happen isn't about forcing anything. Instead, it's about taking initial intentional action, and then being open to inspiration for your next steps.

That means, once you know what you want, you need to intentionally create the systems and structure to get there. This includes creating the channels or opportunities through which you can either receive your desire or move closer to it.

You might create a channel by:

- reaching out to someone who can help you
- starting a new hobby or business that's aligned with your desire
- ending a habit or practice that no longer works for you
- saying yes to an opportunity that comes your way
- following an intuitive nudge

You don't know for sure that any one of these channels will bring your desire closer to manifesting. That's because you can't tell ahead of time exactly how you'll receive your outcome or something that moves you closer to it. What you *do* know is that if you don't create the opportunity, your desire can't manifest through that channel. And taking action is the only way to find out.

If you have a seed that you want to grow into a beautiful flower, you have to take intentional action to help it bloom into its full potential.

Yes, you could just throw the seed out of your window and hope for the best, but if you do this it could end up anywhere. Perhaps you'll get lucky and it will land in a patch of nutritious soil so it can bloom. However, it might just as easily land on a concrete path and never get the chance to grow.

Alternatively, you could take your time, do some research and find the perfect place to intentionally plant the seed. You could find – or create – the perfect soil and choose a place with the right amount of sunshine, shade and protection to plant it. Doing this will give your seed the very best chance of blooming to its fullest.

Being intentional with your choices and actions means actively creating the perfect conditions to receive your desires.

Time to get real

Often, people believe that they're already prioritising what's important to them and being intentional with their time, energy and resources. But when they take a closer look, they realise that they're not being nearly as intentional as they thought.

The quickest way to see how intentional you're being and identify what you're prioritising is to check your calendar and your bank account.

These reflect what you're actually doing with your time and money – and what you do doesn't lie. So if you want to get brutally honest about your priorities, check your diary and bank statements.

Let's take the example of going to the gym that we talked about back in the Introduction. You can have the best intentions around the outcome of getting stronger and fitter by working out regularly at your local gym.

But let's say that when you look back over your calendar, you discover you've never actually booked any workout sessions in. Or maybe you've blocked out times for the sessions, but haven't actually joined a gym and paid for your membership yet. In either of these cases, you're just wishing for the result you want, not consciously using your magick to create it.

In these situations, it's like you're in the canoe from the previous chapter, and everything that doesn't support you is dragging behind you, keeping you from moving forward.

When you check your calendar and bank statements, ask yourself what each one shows about:

- how you're spending your time, money, energy and other resources right now

- how aligned each choice is with supporting your desires

- whether each one reflects your Magickal Life Philosophy

- whether they're supporting you in reclaiming the Magick of You

I know this can be confronting, but it's essential to notice where you're spending your time, energy and resources. Try not to judge or blame yourself if you discover appointments or purchases that aren't helping you to move in the direction you want. Remember that whatever's there, you can only change it once you're aware of it.

Remember too that choosing to consciously, intentionally change the things that don't support you calls back your energy, and with it, your power. It allows you to make the necessary changes to intentionally re-allocate your time, energy and resources in ways that support and align with your desires.

You only have so much money, time, energy and resources available to you. So it's important to spend all of them in a way that aligns with what you actually want in life.

Let's talk about boundaries

To be more intentional in your life, you may have to establish – or re-establish – boundaries with yourself, the activities you do and the people in your life.

The Cambridge dictionary defines a boundary as 'a real or imaginary line that marks the edge or limit of something'. When I talk about boundaries, I mean the line you set that marks the limits of what you will and won't accept in each area of your life.

Setting a clear boundary tells other people what you expect from them. It also reminds you of what you expect from yourself. So you probably need to pay extra attention to your boundaries, and either set or strengthen them, if you notice yourself:

- constantly anticipating other people's needs and prioritising those needs over your own

- feeling unable to say no (or feeling guilty when you say it)

- feeling unsafe about expressing your true thoughts, feelings or desires

- struggling to clearly communicate your needs, or even to *know* what you need

- spending your time, energy and resources on things that don't align with your desires

Boundaries with other people

You can have boundaries in any area of your life, but some of the most common boundaries with other people are emotional, physical, material and intellectual.

Let's explore what each of these boundary types might look like below.

Emotional boundaries: your emotions and feelings

Emotional boundaries protect your right to feel and express your feelings.

These boundaries help you to respond appropriately if someone tries to tell you that your feelings aren't valid, or dismisses you as being 'too emotional' or 'on your period'.

When you have strong emotional boundaries, you expect people to share your excitement as you create an intentional, magickal life. And if people dismiss you or tell you that you're being irrational, your emotional boundaries make it clear that the problem belongs to them, not you.

Physical boundaries: your physical body, time and space

Physical boundaries help to keep you feeling physically safe and comfortable.

They enable you to respond confidently if someone gets so close that you feel uncomfortable, or if they try to touch you in a way that you don't like.

Having strong physical boundaries helps you to ensure that people who come to your home don't overstay their welcome. They also help you to say no to spending time on activities that don't align with your desires.

Material boundaries: your possessions and resources

Material boundaries help to protect the resources you own, and ensure that others respect them too.

They help you to respond when people ask to borrow possessions that you'd rather not lend out. They also support you when other people just help themselves to your things, or borrow them and either don't return them or return them damaged.

And, as we talked about in the section above, strong material boundaries help to ensure that you have the resources you need to pursue your desires.

Intellectual boundaries: your thoughts, opinions and values

Intellectual boundaries help you to own and stand tall in your authentic values and priorities, even if other people don't share them.

Strong intellectual boundaries enable you to hold firm to what you know is true for you when others dismiss your ideas or tell you that your priorities are wrong. They help you to remember that even if someone doesn't honour your request, you still had the right to make it.

These boundaries also enable you to keep moving towards your desires and reconnecting with your magick, whatever others might think.

Boundaries with yourself

In addition to setting boundaries with other people, reclaiming your magick requires you to set strong, clearly defined boundaries with yourself. These boundaries are even more important than the ones you have with others, because they reinforce how much you can trust yourself and honour your own priorities.

Boundaries with yourself help you put the decisions and choices you make into action. They make it easy (or at least easier) to be a person of your word and prioritise your own needs and desires. They also help you to say what you mean and act intentionally, particularly around:

- exercising, eating, sleeping and other health-related intentions

- how you spend your time and money

- how you use the other resources in your life

Remember that you always get to choose how you spend your time, money and other resources. Perhaps you feel like you don't have a choice over some things. You may feel that you *have to* pay rent or utility bills. Actually though, you're choosing to live in the home you're in right now. You're choosing to prioritise access to lighting and heat.

Those are both excellent things to prioritise if living in a safe, healthy, comfortable home is important to you. So I'm not saying you shouldn't choose to spend money on them.

But I'm sure there are plenty of other things you spend your time and money on that don't align with your priorities.

Perhaps you've outgrown them, or perhaps they never truly aligned with your authentic desires in the first place.

Even though these boundaries are with yourself, they may require you to have conversations and make decisions that involve other people.

Perhaps you're emotionally supporting a friend who always takes, takes, takes, and gives very little in return. Or maybe you're financially supporting someone who now relies on your generosity to avoid taking responsibility for themselves.

Withdrawing your support in either case may feel mean and uncaring, but staying true to yourself may make it necessary. You might also need to look at the situation with fresh eyes: are you truly helping this person, or have you allowed them to become too dependent on you?

Setting a boundary in either case might mean becoming more intentional with how you spend your time or money with that friend. That way, if you do keep supporting them, it's because choosing to do so feels aligned, rather than because you're obliged to.

Activity: Examining your boundaries

Look at each of the boundary areas above, and honestly examine how clearly you communicate what's acceptable to you and what's not in that area. For each one, ask yourself:

- Do you actually have a clear boundary (or more than one) in that area? If so, what is it?

- If the boundary is with other people, how easily can you assert that boundary to them?

- If the boundary is with yourself, how easily do you maintain that boundary with yourself?

- How could you make your current boundaries in that area stronger?

- Do you need to set any other, additional boundaries in that area?

Activity: Strengthening your boundaries

Once you've identified all the boundaries you need to strengthen, choose one area of your life to focus on. Start by thinking about who or what pushes that boundary. Then create a plan to support yourself in holding the boundary with that person or situation.

Be aware that it's perfectly normal, especially at the beginning, for creating or maintaining a boundary to feel hard. If this is true for you, you might need some additional support from a coach, counsellor or supportive community.

You need to clearly communicate each boundary, which will probably involve practising how you want to assert it. That way, holding the boundary when you need to becomes easier and more natural. Perhaps you could practise phrases such as:

- "We'll have to disagree on this topic."
- "Please don't do xyz around me anymore."
- "Please step back. You're making me feel uncomfortable."
- "I only have 20 minutes available and then I have to go."
- "Please ask before you take xyz again."
- "You've already asked me that, and I've given you my answer."

These phrases may initially feel uncomfortable, but saying them will become easier over time.

Asserting your boundary doesn't mean you have to be argumentative, but it does mean consciously choosing to initiate the conversations you need to have. Some conversations might happen as and when they arise. For example, if you're sitting at the dinner table and someone says something that violates a boundary for you, you might want to speak up there and then.

For other conversations, the timing might need to be more flexible. In our dinner table example, perhaps tempers get heated and nobody is listening to anyone else. In this case, you might revisit the issue later, once everyone's calmed down and the environment is more conducive to a constructive conversation.

It's important to recognise that a healthy relationship is one where you feel safe asserting your boundaries, and can reasonably expect the other person to respect them. If you're in a situation where that *doesn't* feel safe, you might want to consider reaching out to a professional to support you in deciding the best way forward for you.

The point is that strengthening your boundary requires you to be intentional and choose how you respond to the situation. You need to consciously choose your actions, rather than just ignore the boundary violation and hope it gets better on its own.

Intentional actions are effective actions

Being intentional with your actions isn't always about doing the right thing, doing something perfectly or even knowing what the next action is. But it is about making choices intentionally and not just reacting to life as it happens.

Being intentional is a way of living your life.

The energy you bring to your intentions and your desired outcome weaves into the world to create change. So if your energy, thoughts, words and actions are aligned with your desires, the change you experience will be too.

That means living the Magick of You is a constant energy exchange with the world around you. It's not a demand or a shopping list. There's certainly nothing manipulative about it.

Instead, it's a co-creation with the world around you.

So the more intentional you are with your energy, words, thoughts and actions, the more fulfilled, in flow and on-purpose you'll feel.

Staying intentional

It might sound a bit meta, but you have to stay intentional with your intentionality.

Remaining intentional is something that you have to prioritise as part of your daily routine and everyday habits (again, more about these in *Section 4: Magickal Habits*).

Each day will bring a varying number of competing priorities. So each day, you'll have choices to make. And every choice you make matters. Each choice you make about how you use your time, energy and resources will either move you closer to your desired outcome or move you further away.

Most of these choices, in and of themselves, seem tiny. But the cumulative effect of the hundreds (if not thousands) of choices you make each day creates the results you end up living and experiencing.

That's why it's so important to bring as much intention as you can to each choice you make about how you spend your time, energy and resources. About how you respond to life, the thoughts you focus on and the actions you take.

To start with, this intentionality may feel overwhelming, but it will very quickly become your new normal. As with anything, the more you practise, the easier it becomes.

Ideas to help you focus on remaining intentional include:

- maintaining a clear mental picture of your desired outcome

- being intentional about how you spend your time, money and resources by reviewing each area and making conscious choices

- creating systems and processes that will support you in making those choices

- being intentional with the language you use about your desired outcome

- deliberately choosing who you spend your time with and what you do with them

- consciously choosing the energy you surround yourself with from people, media, events, environments, etc. (see *Chapter 1.3 – Understanding Energy* to remind yourself about these).

Key insights to take with you

- Without an intentional MIND mindset, motivation is nothing more than a good feeling, so it won't help you reclaim your magick on its own.

- Part of taking intentional action is creating opportunities or channels through which you can receive your desires.

- Another part is becoming aware of where you're currently spending time, money and other resources in ways that aren't aligned with the outcome you want.

- Being intentional with your resources often requires setting and holding strong boundaries – both with yourself and other people.

A question to think about

Where do you find it hardest to stay intentional in your life? What resources or support can you draw on to help you become more intentional in that area?

3.4 The Nourished MIND Mindset

Being nourished requires connection

You've set an intention for a desire that you're motivated to achieve, and you've focused your energy by taking aligned action. At this point, the next step is to surrender the outcome of receiving your desire – or something even better – to something bigger than yourself.

This 'something bigger' can go by many names. I've referred to it as 'The Universe' in previous chapters. You might call it 'The Divine', 'Goddess', 'God', 'Spirit' or something completely different. Whatever name you give it, before you can surrender your desire to it, you first need to build and nourish a connection with it.

Nourishing that connection into an ongoing relationship means you can relax, knowing you don't have to manage every last detail of manifesting your desire. It takes away the anxiety and pressure of feeling like you need to control everything to create the outcome you want. And it helps you to trust that, when the waves start to rise and rock your canoe, you'll have all the support you need to navigate them.

Nurturing your relationship with that 'something bigger' is a valuable tool to allow your own divine magick to do its work.

I call my 'something bigger' The Universe

I said above that the name you give your 'something bigger' doesn't matter. This is important enough that I want to repeat it. Some people have grown up learning to call it 'God'. If that's true for you, and that name makes you more comfortable, feel free to keep using it.

Others have had unpleasant, perhaps even abusive, experiences with organised religion. If that's true for you, know that the 'something bigger' I'm talking about is nothing like the vengeful, judgemental God you may have been brought up with. If the name 'God' makes you uneasy, change it to one of the options above, or whatever feels more aligned for you.

Personally, I like to call my 'something bigger' The Universe. That shortens to 'The U', which I lovingly call 'The Big U', because when I say it out loud, it sounds exactly like 'the big you'. This reminds me of my belief that 'The Big U' out there is really just a reflection of the 'little (human) you' down here.

So every time I use the term, it gives me a chance to reflect on the concept of 'as within, so without'. It's a way to remember that I'm connected to, and part of, everything around me.

It also reminds me that I'm not alone.

Again you don't need to change your name for it if you don't want to. But you may find that, like me, referring to your 'something bigger' as 'The Universe' or 'The Big U' helps you to feel part of it.

This is particularly helpful if you've been taught to see nature as 'out there', outside of your home – something that's nice to visit occasionally when you have the time. Thinking of your 'something bigger' as 'The Big U' reminds you that you're not separate from nature.

You're a part of nature.

You *are* nature, in all of its wild, messy, perfectly imperfect glory.

So deepening your relationship with nature – with The Universe – is also deepening your relationship with yourself and your magick. Great relationships are built on trust, and the relationship with The Universe is no different.

Trusting both yourself and The Universe (or whatever you call your 'something bigger'), gives you more confidence in expressing yourself and your own unique blend of magick.

Activity: Exploring the 'something bigger' that's right for you

Take a moment to think, and perhaps journal, about what your experiences with a 'something bigger' were when you were growing up.

- Were you encouraged to build a relationship with a 'something bigger' at all? Or was the idea of anything even vaguely spiritual dismissed or mocked?

- If you were encouraged to build a relationship, was it a nourishing one? Or was it more based on manipulation or fear?

- Were there ways you used to enjoy connecting with your 'something bigger'? If so, what were they?

- Is the 'something bigger' you learnt about as a child still relevant in your life? If not, can you replace it with something that aligns more with your understanding of the world as an adult, and the Magickal Life Philosophy you've chosen?

Next, think about the kind of relationship you'd like with your 'something bigger' today.

- What sort of relationship would you most like to create with it going forward?

- What name would feel most nourishing and supportive to refer to it by?

- What activities would feel most nourishing and supportive to help you create a regular, meaningful connection to it? Perhaps consider:

  - **physical movement**: maybe dancing, yoga, qi gong or walking in nature
  - **sound**: maybe singing, chanting, drumming or spoken prayer
  - **devotional acts**: maybe lighting a candle or undertaking acts of service for others in your community
  - **journaling**: maybe prayer journaling, gratitude journaling or documenting your spiritual journey

Recognise that the way you nourish your connection with your 'something bigger' might well change over time.

That means you don't need to commit to whichever way/s you choose to nourish your connection now for the rest of your life.

As with everything you do to live a magickal life, it's perfectly OK to regularly review your choices and change things up as often as you feel like doing so.

Connection, in turn, needs nourishing

So how do you deepen this relationship with your 'something bigger'? You do so by nourishing it. You can't just continually take. Nor can you just show up when you need something and ignore the relationship the rest of the time.

No one likes to be in those kinds of relationships. As with any other relationship, your relationship with your 'something bigger' is much more fulfilling and supportive if it works both ways.

I wouldn't consider myself religious, but I did grow up in a Christian society. I remember that, at school and on the odd occasions I was taken to church as a child, we recited the Lord's Prayer.

Even if you didn't grow up Christian yourself, you may well have come across this prayer in a TV show or a book you read. It starts with the words 'Our Father, who art in heaven… hallowed be thy name.'

I think of the Lord's Prayer as the way that the people I grew up with nurtured their relationship with their 'something bigger'. Millions of people say this prayer together as part of their religious and spiritual practice. When they repeat the words, they're all doing so for similar reasons.

They say the prayer as part of a ritual. They say it as a form of connection with others who share their beliefs, and with their 'something bigger'. They say it in reverence or recognition of their personal beliefs. They say the words with intention and meaning.

Every time someone says this prayer individually, they add energy to the ritual of prayer generally, and specifically to the prayer that they're saying. When the entire congregation says the prayer together, it magnifies the energy even more.

Each time each person says the prayer, they add their personal energy to its collective power. At the same time, they add energy to their own connection with those words. And as they enhance that connection, they also connect more deeply to their faith and their personal religious and spiritual beliefs.

When we build a relationship with something, we value it more.

People who regularly say the Lord's Prayer build a relationship with it. As they do, they come to value it and the connection it brings them.

Of course, this is true for any prayer from any culture, not just the Lord's Prayer, or other Christian prayers. It's true for any communal ritual, service or act of any faith, religion, culture or group. It's also true for rituals in groups that *aren't* spiritual, for example, the fan groups that form around celebrities, musicians, sports stars or teams, and fictional characters.

And it can even be true of specific songs, stories or poems that are shared in a similar way to a prayer. There's an element of it when the entire audience at a concert, regardless of their different backgrounds, comes together in solidarity to sing a favourite song along with the band on the stage.

Your 'something bigger' doesn't keep score

What if you hadn't created any kind of relationship with your 'something bigger' before you needed help? In that case, you might find the support a lot harder to access.

It's not that I think your 'something bigger' will suddenly decide not to support you. That's not how I'm saying it works. I don't believe in any way that your 'something bigger' keeps score. Nor do I believe that it would deny you support when you needed it, regardless of whether you'd built a relationship with it or not.

But *you'd* know that the relationship didn't exist.

It's much easier to ask for something if you've built and nurtured a relationship with someone. All relationships – whether they're with a 'something bigger', a family member, a colleague or a friend – work better when you nourish them and give them your time and energy.

If you're constantly taking from a relationship, at some point you'll start to feel awkward and then perhaps just stop asking. If this happens, you'll likely find it harder to access the available support from your 'something bigger'. You just won't have the same level of trust that it will be there for you.

But when you've created a nourishing relationship with your 'something bigger', you feel a deep knowing that it will support you in your endeavours. You set intentions and confidently release them to it, knowing that it's on your side.

You slowly start to expect that things will work out in your favour, even if you don't quite understand how in the moment. You look for signs and synchronicities, trusting that they're nods from your 'something bigger' that you're on the right track.

Once you've built your relationship, you're comfortable expecting it to meet you halfway.

That foundation allows you to relax, knowing that you don't need to micromanage every step of your life. You can surrender the outcome you desire to your 'something bigger', and when you say, "Thank you. This or something better," you truly believe it.

Nourishing your relationship with your 'something bigger' allows you to step into its flow and simply trust.

Rituals deepen your connection

The more often you do or say something, the more power and energy you add to that action.

In the same way, the more you participate in a relationship-building process, the deeper and more meaningful the relationship will become. Repeating a supportive action or ritual within a relationship will gradually bring a feeling of support into the relationship itself.

The very first flat I lived in had its electricity on a meter system. When you put a 50p coin in the meter's slot, it would turn on the electricity.

If you used up the electricity you'd bought with your 50p coins, it would immediately stop. And yes, that did happen to me once while I was in the shower. So you can bet that I always kept the meter topped up fully from then on!

That meter is a great symbol of the strength of your connection with yourself, your magick and your 'something bigger'. Everything you do to nourish your relationship with your 'something bigger' adds a 50p coin to your meter. Then, every time you draw on the relationship for help or support with something, you use up some of the electricity you've bought from the meter.

The 50p coins you add to this meter come from activities that nurture your relationship with The Universe. I've listed some of the possible activities you could use to do this in the exercise earlier in this chapter, but you might well be able to think of others.

And if the activity you choose is a communal one – a collective prayer or ritual – you're not just topping up your own electricity meter. You're also topping up the collective meter of everyone who shares in the same ritual.

So when the day comes that you need help, guidance or support, your electricity meter is fully charged. Knowing this gives you a sense of being fully supported in making your desire a reality. The time and energy you've put into building the relationship allow you to trust that you'll receive back some of what you've put in.

As a result, you feel confident in your ability to draw on this collective energy.

In the example of repeating the Lord's Prayer, you've been building your personal relationship with the Christian God. You've added to the energy of your relationship by showing your devotion in the form of prayer, and possibly in other ways too.

Then, when you need help, support or guidance, you ask God for it through the act of prayer. Perhaps you go to a formal service or seek out the counsel of a vicar or priest. And you have faith that God will support and guide you.

Again, this is true across all faiths and religions, not just Christianity. It's particularly true for the many people who draw great comfort from rituals, ceremonies and rites of passage at times of upheaval and change.

Connection can also strengthen over generations

When you nourish your relationship with your 'something bigger', the support you can access isn't limited to the 50p coins you've put in the meter yourself. Nor is it limited to the coins that the community you practise together with has put in to top up the collective meter.

You can also draw on the connections that generations before you have created and nourished. These connections can extend to those that your heritage, your family, your culture and your society have built as well.

If your family, culture or lineage has done something for generations before you, they've created a foundation of support that you can draw on. When you participate in the same practices and traditions that they've used over and over again, you're adding to that foundation. You're topping up an electricity meter that extends back through the generations.

And you're topping up your trust that when you need support, it will be there for you.

So every time you pray, sing or chant something you learnt as a tradition, you tap into its universal energy. The same is true when you share a story, poem or psalm, and when you drum, dance or light a candle too. In fact, any time you intentionally use a practice drawn from a shared heritage that has meaning to you, you connect with an energy that's bigger than you.

That's exactly why ritual is so powerful and comforting to so many people from so many cultures.

Practising these rituals can remind you that you're never alone. It also allows you to draw on the love and support of all those who came before you, regardless of your current relationship with your family of origin.

You can create your own rituals too

Rituals don't have to be cultural practices handed down through generations. At any point, for any reason, you can create your own.

How you create your connection with your 'something bigger' is completely up to you.

In 2018, I dedicated as a Priestess of Cerridwen on the shores of Lake Bala in Wales.

And now, every day, I deepen my connection with her in different ways. Sometimes it's through rituals and offerings. Other times, it's simply through giving a cheeky wink to one of the statues I have around my home.

For me, deepening the connection isn't a religious undertaking. It's certainly not a dogmatic one. Instead, it's a personal activity. And I believe that only you will know what feels right and appropriate to you in nourishing your own relationship.

We'll talk more about exactly how to create powerful rituals that have personal meaning and significance to you in *Section 5: Magickal Practices*. But before you start doing that, you need to understand the final element of a magickal MIND mindset, along with the building blocks of rituals – magickal habits.

So bear with me as we cover the last few basics over the coming chapters.

Staying nourished

Creating and nourishing a relationship with 'your something bigger' is an ongoing process that needs time, energy and attention. Sometimes it will take a lot of your time, and other times just a little. As with all relationships, though, you very much get what you put in.

At some times in your life, you might create and nourish a daily connection with your 'something bigger'. During other times, your connection may be less frequent. You might create your own personal rituals or tap into the energy of collective ones – and again, we'll discuss this more in *Section 5: Magickal Practices.*

In the meantime, ideas to keep nourishing your relationship with your 'something bigger' include:

- building an altar to connect with it (or just choosing a single object)

- lighting a candle in its honour

- praying or just casually talking to it

- journaling about your relationship with it

- asking it for guidance, and asking what you can do for it too

- meditating or spending time in nature to deepen your connection with it

Key insights to take with you

- A Nourished MIND mindset is all about building and nurturing a relationship with 'something bigger' than you, whatever name you give it.

- I like to call my 'something bigger' The Universe, or The Big U ('big you'), because it reminds me that I'm a smaller reflection of it.

- Nourishing your relationship with your 'something bigger' makes it easier to draw on and trust in the support that The Universe offers.

- Allowing yourself to draw on that support means you don't have the pressure of micromanaging every minute detail of bringing your desire into reality.

A question to think about

When you think of your ideal 'something bigger', how do you imagine it? How do you imagine it supporting you in living your magickal life?

3.5 The Dedicated MIND Mindset

Staying on track takes dedication

You're motivated and clear on your why. You're being intentional with your time, energy and resources. You've nourished your connection with your 'something bigger' and feel supported and confident that it will meet you halfway in manifesting your desire. But there's one last step you need to take to keep you on track with your Magickal MIND mindset.

You need to dedicate yourself to maintaining it.

Once you've consciously chosen your desired outcome and done the practical work, it's important to dedicate yourself to holding space to receive the outcome.

This means making a powerful choice to prioritise yourself and your magick.

It also means showing up consistently in your energy, thoughts and actions.

When you dedicate yourself to something, it becomes non-negotiable. You declare its importance in your life. You prepare yourself to prioritise it over other things.

Dedication helps you to overcome busyness, discomfort and doubt, or at least it helps you to refuse to let them stop you. It means you commit to showing up each and every day, even when you don't feel like it or it's inconvenient.

When you dedicate yourself to your work, your magick and your desired outcome, you remain true to yourself above all else.

You raise your standards and expectations of yourself, of other people and of life itself.

Dedication doesn't mean you're forever trapped

Some people worry that if they take that extra step of dedicating themselves to a goal, it means they can't ever change their minds. They fear that, instead of being a support structure for achieving their desire, dedication will create a cage that traps them in striving towards a goal that's no longer relevant.

I like to think of this as a bit like being in a long-term relationship – perhaps even a marriage – with your desire. After all, people do talk about being 'wedded to a goal'.

Getting married means making a long-term commitment to another person. It means agreeing to do your best to make the relationship with your spouse work for as long as the relationship is right and healthy for both of you.

But, as I've said many times already in this book, things can change. If you both grow in very different directions over time, the relationship may no longer be right the way it was when you made the commitment. So, after a lot of soul-searching, you might decide that the time has come to separate.

The same is true with your desire. It's OK to take a step back from something you've dedicated yourself to, recognise that it's no longer the right path for you and let it go.

Just make sure you do put some real consideration into making that decision. Changing your mind about a goal you've dedicated yourself to should be like getting a divorce, not ghosting a blind date!

The difference between decision and dedication

I've often been asked about the difference between deciding to do something and dedicating yourself to that outcome. The way I see it, dedicating yourself to something feels more powerful than just simply making a decision.

I said in *Chapter 3.3 – The Intentional MIND Mindset* that we all make hundreds, if not thousands, of decisions every day. Some of those we stick to. Others we don't.

But dedicating ourselves to something has more gravitas. It has more meaning.

I initially *decided* that I wanted to train to be a Priestess of Cerridwen. Then, at the end of the training, I *dedicated* as a Priestess of Cerridwen to show my commitment to walking that path.

Dedicating yourself to something takes the clear intention you set earlier and strengthens it, both for yourself and for the wider world.

A dedication makes that intention non-negotiable.

Continuing with our theme of relationships above, you might *decide* to agree to a date with someone you enjoy spending time with. You might even *decide* that you're in love with your partner, and you'd like the relationship to be a long-term one.

But if you then decide to get married or create a civil partnership, you're both consciously committing and *dedicating* yourself to the relationship.

You move as a couple from simply being in love – a state that may be temporary – to making a legally binding commitment. You and your partner dedicate yourselves to each other, often in front of family and friends. You promise to always be there for each other, to love each other and support each other.

Of course, you don't have to be married to dedicate yourself to a romantic partner. Still, the enormity of the wedding industry shows just how important this ritual of commitment and dedication is to people in our society.

Ritual can support your dedication

We talked about how ritual can support connection in the previous chapter, but it can also support your dedication. That's why formal dedications are often accompanied by some kind of ceremony or ritual that adds to the situation's gravitas.

When I dedicated as a Priestess of Cerridwen together with the other members of my group, we enhanced our dedication with a ritual that was meaningful to us.

We prepared ourselves for the event by completing ritual bathing, and wearing special clothes and jewellery. We meditated, chanted, drummed, walked a labyrinth and then stepped out into Lake Bala at sunset to speak our vows of dedication.

It was a significant event that we invited others to witness, and swarms of midges witnessed it uninvited: a trial of dedication in itself!

Dedicating yourself to your intention doesn't *have* to be that dramatic. But if you've set a substantial intention that will demand your focus and attention for a while, you might consider performing a small ceremony to mark your dedication.

This could be as simple as lighting a candle and writing down what you're dedicating to, then signing and dating it. Or, if it feels right, you could make the ritual more elaborate. I've provided some ideas in the activity later in this chapter. You can also ask other people to witness the ritual if that feels appropriate and you know those people will support you.

But the most important thing is making a contract of dedication with yourself. You'll find some ideas for doing this in Step 3 of the Dedicating to the Magick of You activity later in this chapter.

Creating a tangible symbol of your dedication

As an alternative to a ritual – or perhaps in addition to it – I think it's fun to buy or create something that reminds you of your dedication. Seeing this physical symbol of your dedication can help to keep your intention front and centre of your mind.

If you enjoy making things, you might create a small figurine or other object that feels meaningful to you as a symbol of your dedication. If you sew, weave or do some form of fibre craft, you might make a scarf or other piece of clothing for yourself. Or, if you're artistic, you might draw or paint something that represents the outcome you're dedicating yourself to.

Creating something yourself is always powerful, but you don't have to do this if it doesn't feel aligned for you. You might instead dedicate a piece of jewellery to symbolise your intention. This can either be a piece you already own, or a new piece you've bought specifically.

Then, every day you wear that jewellery, it will remind you of your intention and your dedication to manifesting it.

A powerful everyday example of jewellery as a symbol of dedication is a wedding ring. Couples who dedicate themselves to each other exchange rings in many cultures throughout the world. The rings represent the eternity of a circle, so they carry the association of marriage and commitment.

Again, the symbol you choose doesn't have to be jewellery. It could be a special perfume or an accessory or article of clothing that you wear. Then, every time you apply it or slip it on, it will remind you of your dedication.

Perhaps you could buy a crystal, or a small statue, or something else meaningful and place it somewhere you'll see it regularly to deepen your dedication.

If you wanted to get really creative, you could write your dedication on the bottom of your shoes (with a suitable non-floor-staining pen). That way, you'd know that every step you took would activate your dedication. It's not about seeing the ink or reading the words in this case. Instead, it's about knowing that you've dedicated literally walking your path to manifesting your intention.

Dedicating your environment to your success

When was the last time you thought about how your environment supports you, not just in manifesting a particular intention, but in your overall success?

In *Chapter 3.3 – the Intentional MIND Mindset*, I talked about creating the right conditions for success. And over the previous chapters in this section, I've also discussed the importance of *keeping* your Magickal MIND mindset in place once you've created it.

Part of dedicating yourself to the success of your intention is setting up the right conditions around you to support that success.

This includes drawing on the power of magickal habits, which we'll talk about more in the next section of this book. But it also includes your physical environment.

Dedicating your environment to your success means making the things you need to create that success easier to access. It also means making distractions harder to access.

For example, let's say that your desire is to feel fitter and healthier. The aligned action you've decided to take is to start running three mornings a week. As part of dedicating your environment to success, you could lay out your running gear on the chair beside your bed each evening before a scheduled run. This has two benefits:

1. It means you see your running gear first thing when you wake up, which reminds you that, oh yes, you'd intended to go running this morning.
2. You also reduce the number of actions you need to take once you've woken up to prepare for your run.

Leaving it till the morning of your run to get your running gear out might not sound like a very big action. Especially first thing in the morning, though, the little things count. Given half a chance, it's all too easy to forget that you'd intended to go running. It's easy to decide that something else needs to take priority today, and promise yourself you'll run tomorrow instead.

And in that 'first thing in the morning' mind state, having to actively dig your gear out before you can put it on can feel like a much bigger job than it really is. If you see your running gear sitting there, waiting for you as soon as you wake up, though, that's one less reason you have not to go.

Alternatively, let's say your goal is to spend your time more intentionally – perhaps because you want to dedicate more time to your spiritual practice. Perhaps the aligned action you've decided to take is to reduce the amount of time you spend scrolling social media on your phone, or news sites on your computer.

In this situation, setting your environment up for success might involve:

- using the tools on your phone to either block social media apps altogether, or intentionally limit your time on them

- setting up a browser blocker on your computer that again, either completely blocks or limits the time you can spend on news sites

- setting your browser's home page as something that supports your intention, perhaps a meditation website, or the homepage for a course you're doing right now

It's important to note that doing these things isn't about making news or social media 'bad'. It's just about recognising that they don't support you in achieving your current desire. And then, once you've recognised this, it's about setting up your environment so you find it easier to break old habits, and make more supportive choices instead.

These acts of dedication, no matter how small, focus you on your growth and create momentum towards your desired outcome.

Activity: Dedicating to the Magick of You

If you'd like to complete a formal ritual to dedicate yourself to the Magick of You, this activity will give you some ideas to create one. Of course, as with everything else in this book, feel free to tailor it to whatever feels right for you.

Things you may want to include

As symbols of your dedication, you might want to use:

- an altar containing items that represent your magick or values that are important to you

- objects for your altar that represent the elements, for example:

  - for Air, you might use a feather or some incense

  - for Earth, a crystal or a bowl of sand or earth

  - for Fire, a candle

  - for Water, a small bowl of water

- a candle (in addition to your symbol of Fire, if you have one)
- a pen and paper – these could be special writing tools, your journal and favourite pen, or just whatever you have to hand

Step 1. Create your sacred space

Light your candle if you're using one, and set the intention to connect deeply with the Magick of You.

If you're using symbols of the elements, you might also want to invoke or acknowledge each element in some way.

Step 2. Connect with the Magick of You

Spend some time connecting with the Magick of You. Imagine how it would feel to live a more magickal life that aligns with what's truly important to you.

Then get clear on what your desired outcome is for this moment in time, and what dedication you'll need to make to bring it into reality.

Step 3. Write your contract of dedication

Use the writing tools you've chosen to create your contract of dedication.

This could be as short as a couple of lines, or end up being a full page of all the ways you're going to dedicate yourself to your magick.

In the contract, include everything you're dedicating yourself to so that you can achieve the outcome you desire. Ideas to consider include:

- being loyal to yourself and your magick
- being honest with yourself
- asking for help when you need it
- asserting your boundaries where appropriate
- reviewing your intentions regularly
- nourishing your relationship with your 'something bigger'
- making time and resources available for your desire
- being disciplined in your actions
- creating habits to support you

Finally, date and sign your contract.

You could even get a trusted friend to witness it for you, but this isn't necessary.

Staying dedicated

Once you've dedicated yourself to the outcome you desire, it's essential to then back your dedication up with some kind of action. Again, it's the action that makes all the difference.

Many people feel that they've already dedicated themselves to their desire. But unless their actions reflect their dedication, all they've done is set an intention.

To help you stay dedicated you could:

- create a clear vision of the outcome and spend time visualising it each day

- create an actionable plan to get to your desired outcome and break it down into smaller steps

- spend time getting clear on additional support you may need to manifest your desire

- commit to taking daily action towards your outcome, no matter how small it might be

- light a candle each day in honour of your dedication

- pull a daily oracle card to offer guidance on your dedication and actions to get you there

- make changes to create the right environment to support you

Key insights to take with you

- Staying on track with your intention requires dedicating yourself to the outcome you desire.

- A dedication is more significant and has more gravitas to it than a decision.

- You can support your dedication by creating a ritual around it that's as simple or elaborate as you want it to be.

- You can also support your dedication by creating a physical symbol of it as a reminder, and by setting up your environment to encourage you to make supportive choices.

A question to think about

Which elements of your environment already support you in dedicating yourself to your desired outcome? Which elements don't, and how could you change them?

3.6 Magickal MIND Mindset Compromisers

Struggling to maintain a Magickal MIND mindset?

I don't believe in sugar-coating reality, so I'm not going to tell you that maintaining a Magickal MIND mindset is always easy. There are so many things that can knock your mindset off track. Some of these issues – usually physical – are obvious, such as:

- lack of sleep
- background stress
- having a cold or some other minor illness
- minor physical pain or discomfort
- feeling hungry

These are immediate, in-the-moment things that are often easy to fix once you become aware of them. Then, as soon as you've addressed the issue, it generally doesn't affect you as much anymore (at least until the next time).

Then there are more complex, long-term situations that people may find themselves in, which will inevitably affect their mindset. These things are too complex for this book to cover effectively, and often need more specialist support, for example:

- chronic illness or pain

- job loss

- grieving a loved one

- food or housing insecurity

Whilst a Magickal MIND mindset may help a little in these situations, sometimes your own magick just isn't enough to make things better. In these cases, you need the support of community, trained professionals, and sometimes, wider system changes.

In fact, no matter how much you want to rely on your own personal magick, sometimes true power lies in recognising when something's beyond your ability to resolve on your own. For those situations, embodying your magick is about gathering the courage to reach out and call on the experience and expertise of doctors, therapists and professional or community organisations.

Beyond this, there are also far more subtle factors that can influence your mindset – things that you might not be aware of. These are the negative patterns and limiting beliefs that you've learnt or inherited. These patterns or beliefs can make you feel as though you're not good enough, helpless, overwhelmed, fearful or ashamed.

So in this chapter, I want to very quickly cover four of the most common patterns and beliefs that I see routinely compromising the mindsets of my clients. If you find you can relate to any of them, I've also suggested an activity to try when you notice yourself caught up in them.

I want to acknowledge, though, that in some situations, the process of untangling a belief or pattern can be more complex. I've specifically designed some of the practices and rituals in *Section 5: Magickal Practices* to help you separate out what's genuinely yours from what isn't. So you may find those practices helpful in letting go of these patterns too.

Compromiser 1: Being stuck in the role of the good girl

Trying to please everyone around you always fails. You can't possibly please all of the people all of the time. Of course, that doesn't stop a 'good girl' from trying.

That's because part of being a good girl is trying to keep everyone around you happy.

Being a good girl often means saying yes to things that you don't really want to do, and finding it difficult to say no. And as we discussed in *Chapter 3.3 – The Intentional MIND Mindset*, struggling to say no is a clear sign that you need to establish stronger boundaries.

When it comes to mindset, poor boundaries are an issue because they make it almost impossible to reclaim your magick and create what you want in your life. Instead of cultivating the power and passion of your creativity, you use that same energy to burn down and destroy your own dreams.

As a result, you end up feeling exhausted, burnt out and resentful. It's not a physical or mental state that's conducive to a Magickal MIND mindset.

Having poor boundaries also means that no matter how big or small your desire is, you'll struggle to consistently hold its energy. It will keep leaking out of your life like a magickal potion from a cracked cauldron.

Activity: Letting go of your inner good girl

Being a good girl doesn't make you a good person. It's more important to have clear, strong boundaries than it is to have everyone like you.

To help you experience the freedom of letting go of your inner good girl:

1. Pick one of the boundaries with other people that we discussed in *Chapter 3.3 – The Intentional MIND Mindset*, either:

   - emotional
   - physical
   - material
   - intellectual

   Or choose a boundary with yourself if you prefer.

2. Give yourself an imaginary credit of £50, or the equivalent in your country's currency, for the coming week.

3. Over the next week, every time you assert or maintain your chosen boundary, give yourself an extra credit:

   - £5 for each time you say no and hold your boundary when it's fairly easy to do

   - £10 for each time you say no and hold your boundary when you feel as though you 'should' say yes, but know that wouldn't align with your Magickal Life Philosophy

4. At the same time, over the next week, notice when you *don't* maintain your boundary, and deduct:

   - £5 when you do something you didn't want to do because it was easier to just 'go with the flow'

   - £10 when you do something you didn't want to out of obligation because you felt you really had to

5. Each night, check in with yourself and reflect back over how you did with honouring your boundaries, and where you struggled.

6. Finally, at the end of the week, total up your imaginary credit score to see how you did.

   - If you're still in credit, and perhaps even better off than when you started, congratulations! Keep up the good work.

   - If you went into overdraft, acknowledge yourself for doing this exercise and for having the courage to identify where you can plan to make improvements. Use the boundary-strengthening activity in *Chapter 3.3 – The Intentional MIND Mindset* to help with this if you need to.

Compromiser 2: Feeling guilty for every negative thought or feeling

It's easy to believe you don't have your desire because you've been having negative thoughts about something, and then blame yourself for it. After all, common wisdom amongst spiritual-but-not-religious types is that manifesting your desires requires exclusively focusing on the positive.

The problem is that you'll always have *some* negative thoughts and feelings. You're human, and it's what our human minds have evolved to do. Not to mention that sometimes, feeling bad can be a bright, flashing sign from your inner wisdom that points to something you've been tolerating that you're now ready to change.

Regardless, blaming yourself for being human is toxic behaviour. The toxicity is even greater when someone else shames you for not having your desire by telling you it's because you didn't stay positive enough.

No, constant negativity isn't good for you, but believing that a single off-day or a few negative thoughts can stop you from creating what you want isn't helpful either. Thinking or feeling something negative doesn't make you a bad person. Nor does it instantly attract negative energy or situations towards you.

So instead of focusing on staying positive, focus on being honest with yourself about your thoughts and feelings. You don't need to dwell on something that's not going well, but you're allowed to acknowledge your genuine feelings around it.

Remember: having an off-day (or more than one) makes you human. The Universe doesn't punish you for every negative thought you have by taking away the things you desire.

To help you get more comfortable with having the odd negative thought:

1. Think of a negative thought you've had recently. Perhaps it was about yourself or a situation you experienced.

    Maybe you burnt the breakfast toast this morning, so you thought 'I'm completely hopeless at everything. I can't even make toast!'

2. Ask yourself, "Is this actually true?" This question doesn't deny your experience or cover it over with a positive thought. It recognises the truth of your experience, while inviting you to explore the reality of what it means.

    In the case of burning toast, you might recognise that you've made breakfast hundreds of other times successfully in the past. You might also remind yourself that even if you *couldn't* make toast, it wouldn't make you 'completely hopeless'. You've probably done many, many other non-toast-related things successfully.

3. Explore what you could do to stop the situation that prompted the negative thought from happening again.

    While everyone makes mistakes sometimes, that doesn't mean you want to keep making the same ones over and over. In our toast example, perhaps you could make a note to check the timer on the toaster before putting the bread in for future breakfasts.

Compromiser 3: Worrying about being judged

Fear of what other people think of you can create a powerful block that prevents you from claiming what you truly want.

When you don't trust yourself, you can't create from a foundation of security and safety. And constantly looking outside of yourself for validation keeps you from truly trusting yourself and owning your inner power.

To maintain a Magickal MIND mindset, you have to bring your whole self into the process. As I said in *Chapter 2.2 – Getting Full of Yourself*, you can't just embody the parts that make other people feel comfortable.

Activity: Letting go of the fear of judgement

No one can tell you what you should create in your life with your magick. You have to discover what's genuinely right for you for yourself.

Take some time to journal around the following questions:

- What's something you're doing right now because you think you should do it or because it's expected of you, and not because it aligns with your Magickal Life Philosophy?

- If I could wave my magick wand to make it happen for you, what would you most like to do, be or have?

- Write down somewhere between five and ten things you'd change in your life if you had no fear of being judged.

- What's one bold action you could take to start making one of these things happen?

- Imagine someone judges you for prioritising yourself and your desires. What are three constructive, helpful ways you could respond?

Compromiser 4: Being stuck in good vibes only

The flip side of feeling guilty for your negative thoughts or feelings is pretending that they don't exist at all. Denying that challenging events are happening doesn't change reality. It just buries your feelings about them deep within you where they can fester and compromise your mindset.

Life is beautiful and magnificent. It's also hard and unjust.

Trying to maintain a good-vibes-only attitude ignores the truth of life. It's a 'spiritual bypass' that deprives you of the ability to heal from the situation, grow and make your life (and maybe even the world) a bit better.

Reclaiming your magick isn't some kind of superficial quick fix. It's a way of building a life that supports you choice by choice. Just focusing on the ra-ra-ra jazz hands of life doesn't create lasting change. At best, it puts a temporary, and very superficial, sticking plaster over the authentic pain and struggles you experience.

Activity: Letting go of good vibes only

One of the most common places you'll see a good-vibes-only mentality play out is around anger.

The emotion of anger often gets a bad rap. It's frequently labelled as bad or seen as a sign that you're out of control.

But anger can be sacred. It can be a powerful tool for transformation. So if you notice there's something in the external world that you're angry about, don't try to push it down and pretend everything's fine. Instead...

1. Write out the thing that made you angry, including everything that comes to mind about the situation. Don't spare any details or worry about hurting people's feelings. No one will see what you've written.

2. Once you've written as much as you need to, burn the paper somewhere safe and suitable – for example, in a fire-proof pot, a cauldron or a hearth.

3. As the paper burns, feel the energy of Fire transforming your anger into something sacred.

4. Let the paper burn fully, and relight it if you need to. Sometimes you might need to relight it several times if the flame struggles to burn. If this happens, ask yourself whether this reflects you struggling to let go of the anger.

5. Take some time to sit and reflect on your experience. Ask yourself what action you need to take to honour your sacred anger. This might be:

- starting to do something differently (or stopping something you've been doing)
- having a difficult conversation with someone
- setting or reaffirming a boundary

Listen for the voice of your intuition to tell you what the action needs to be. Remind yourself of what this is likely to sound like in *Chapter 1.2 – The Role of Intuition* if you need to.

Remember that the answer might come immediately... but it might also present itself to you as an intuitive insight or inspiration over the next few days.

If you prefer not to write

If you don't want to write anything down or don't have anywhere suitable to burn your paper, you can still transform your anger.

Instead of using literal fire, you can dance, drum or sweat to create the energy of Fire. Feel the anger in your body, and then feel the Fire energy burning inside you. Feel it consuming the anger, transforming it so it leaves your body.

Again, once you've done this, follow Step 5 above to identify what action you need to take to honour your anger.

Key insights to take with you

- Maintaining a Magickal MIND mindset is something you need to keep doing, as several factors can compromise it.

- Some of these compromisers are simple and quick to deal with in the moment, but others are more subtle and long-term.

- Sometimes, it may be enough to simply recognise that these subtle mindset compromisers don't reflect your objective truth, but other times it may take more work.

- The activities in this chapter provide some mindset compromiser quick fixes – but if you need more help, you'll find practices and rituals in *Section 5: Magickal Practices*.

A question to think about

Which of these mindset compromisers is most familiar to you? What tools (beyond the activities in this chapter) can you access to help you manage it?

3.7 If You're Still Struggling with Mindset

Real talk: are you focusing on ALL the mindset elements?

As I said in the previous chapter, maintaining a Magickal MIND mindset can be challenging. If you've worked through all the activities in that chapter, but can still feel your mindset slumping, it might be time to take a step back and check in with yourself.

It's easy to feel like you're doing all the things you need to do to keep your mindset magickal on the surface. Meanwhile, somewhere, deep down, you're ignoring something essential.

The thing you're ignoring might be something about the desire you're trying to manifest. It might be something about your authentic self and your connection to your 'something bigger'. Or it might be something about your life and current priorities, and how the outcome you want to manifest fits in with them.

If you immediately know where the problem lies, I'd recommend going back and reading the chapter that feels most relevant to it. But if nothing jumps out at you, I suggest working through the questions in this chapter to help you hone in on the root issue... and what to do about it.

Review your motivation for the desire itself

Before you do anything else, ask yourself whether you're still truly motivated to work towards this desire. Remind yourself that there's no right or wrong answer to this question, as long as you're honest with yourself.

Changing your mind doesn't make you wrong or a failure. Nor does it mean that the desire you focused on was wrong to start with.

As you've spent time working towards your desire, no doubt you've changed and grown. Perhaps your environment or situation has changed too. So while this desire might have been something you were genuinely motivated to manifest at the beginning, that might not be true anymore.

Maybe you've outgrown your desire now. Maybe it's just not as important to you today as it was then. Or perhaps you still want it, but you no longer have the same ability to work towards it as you had when you started.

As we discussed in *Chapter 3.5 – The Dedicated MIND Mindset*, being able and willing to reassess your desire doesn't make you indecisive or flaky. It makes you someone with enough experience to know that you, your desires and your life are all constantly changing. As they do, you need to be flexible and adaptable enough to respond appropriately.

Additionally, sometimes, you might really believe that you want a particular outcome. But then, once you start taking action towards it, you quickly realise that this dream wasn't yours to begin with. It was just what someone else wanted for you, and you'd internalised it as your own.

Other times, you might discover that the reality of the outcome simply wasn't what you expected.

Either way, you may not need to abandon your desire completely. Perhaps it just needs a slight change to reflect your priorities and values now. Then again, perhaps it's no longer right for you on any level.

If the first option is true, you might find that as soon as you make that change, your mindset magickally recovers. If, on the other hand, you discover that the desire is no longer right at all, you can stop wasting your time, energy and resources on it.

Instead, you can ask yourself what you really do want, refocus on that and then set off again.

As hard as it may be to hear, we're not meant to realise ALL of our dreams and desires. Sometimes, even the ones we think we want with our whole hearts simply arise so that we can start taking actions to change in a certain way.

These actions then often set us on the path to discovering what we really want.

Assess how intentional your actions are

If you're still certain about your motivation for your desires, review how intentional you've been with your time, energy and resources.

Have you been blocking out time to consciously work towards your desire? Have you connected with others who can support you? Have you researched different ways to achieve your outcome or face the internal or external challenges you encounter?

Check back through your diary and bank account again. Look at how you've been allocating your resources. Do they reflect how much you want your outcome?

Have you been prioritising the actions you need to take to move forward? Or has your desire got lost in the busyness of life?

If other things in your life have taken over, don't shame or blame yourself for it. Just acknowledge what's happened, and then refocus and get intentional again. Commit to prioritising your progress in what's really important to you.

At the same time, remember that any progress – no matter how small – is still progress. It still deserves celebrating. Many of us tend to overestimate what we can do in a short time span, and then make ourselves wrong for not achieving it.

Make sure you're not being too hard on yourself. It's always OK to readjust your expectations.

And remember that every choice you make is an opportunity to get back on track and become intentional again. You don't need to wait for Monday, or even tomorrow. You can make your very next choice count.

Check your connection with your 'something bigger'

If you're still motivated and you're taking regular intentional action, it's time to check in with how much you're allowing your 'something bigger' to support you.

Are you working together *with* it to bring the outcome you want into reality? Or are you trying to control and micromanage every eventuality?

Stepping into the energy of control is exhausting. It's also a waste of your precious time, because there's no way that you can possibly control every person and event around you.

When you don't trust that your 'something bigger' is working with you, you become rigid and hyper-focused on how your desired outcome will eventuate. This cuts you off from recognising other opportunities that appear, and that may be a better fit for you.

Think back over your life. I'm sure some of your most incredible experiences – maybe a relationship or a promotion – came along when you hadn't expected or planned for them. But no doubt you were ready for them when they arrived.

Perhaps without knowing it's what you were doing, you'd put the work in to prepare yourself for them. You were open to receiving the outcome, even if you weren't consciously looking for it.

And the way it showed up in your life wasn't anything you'd imagined in your wildest dreams.

That's exactly how nourishing your relationship with your 'something bigger' works. You get clear on what you want, do your part and then remain open to receiving it, trusting that it will come your way.

Evaluate your dedication to your desire

Finally, if you're comfortable with your level of focus on the other three elements of a Magickal MIND mindset, it's time to check your commitment to making it happen.

Do you still feel dedicated to your desired outcome? If so, what changes have you made to reflect that dedication?

How have you set up your environment to support you?

How have you made it easy for yourself to take regular – perhaps even daily – action?

Without regular action to externalise your dedication, it's natural to get complacent around your commitment to your desire.

It's a bit like being in a new relationship. To start with, both partners are on their best behaviour. They're intensely considerate of each other, prioritising each other's happiness. As time goes by, though, the initial novelty wears off. Slowly, they can find themselves paying less and less attention to each other.

In the same way, without paying continuous attention to your desire, it's easy to stop focusing on your dedication to it. A little less attention gradually becomes a lot less attention. Before long, the outcome you dedicated yourself to just doesn't feel that important anymore.

Assuming that it *is* still important, which you checked earlier in the chapter, it's time to recommit and re-dedicate yourself to your desire and make it a genuine priority once more.

Activity: Magickal MIND mindset check-in cheat sheet

Whenever you find yourself not getting the mindset results you desire, ask yourself...

Are you MOTIVATED?

Do you really want the outcome that you say you do?

Are you clear on WHY you want it?

Are you emotionally invested in it, or is it just something 'nice' to do?

Are you taking INTENTIONAL action?

When you observe your thoughts, words and actions, do they align with the outcome you desire?

Are you making choices that intentionally support your progress?

What do your calendar and your bank statement say about your priorities?

Are you feeling NOURISHED?

Does your relationship with your 'something bigger' feel nourished?

Are you contributing to the relationship, or does it feel depleted because you're only taking?

Are you open to accepting support from your 'something bigger', or are you trying to micromanage everything on your own?

Are you truly DEDICATED?

Have you really dedicated yourself to the outcome
you desire?

Are you regularly taking actions that move you closer
to your desired outcome, even if it's sometimes hard or
inconvenient for those around you?

Have you set up your environment to make it as easy as
possible to take those actions?

Key insights to take with you

- Maintaining all of the elements of a Magickal MIND
  mindset can be challenging, and it's easy to let one (or
  more) of them slip over time.

- When this happens, this chapter offers some suggestions
  for getting your mindset back on track again.

- The key to staying on course doesn't lie in being perfect,
  but instead in accepting that drifting off course is natural,
  and then taking action to recommit when you do.

A question to think about

Which element of your mindset tends to reliably
'fall over' the quickest? What can you do to help that
happen less often?

Section 4: **Magickal Habits**

The day-to-day actions and habits that help you to reconnect with, reclaim and embody your magick

4.1 Magickal Habits for a More Magickal You

Why look at habits?

To build the foundation for living and expressing the Magick of You, it's essential to look at your habits. That's because, simply put, habits are the decisions you no longer think about making.

Yes, you can consciously decide to create a habit. At least for a while, you may also need to continue consciously deciding to take actions that keep the habit going.

Eventually, though, when the habit kicks in, it runs on automatic.

The trick is that not every habit starts in response to a conscious decision. Of those that don't, some will support you in reclaiming your magick and creating the life you want. Others will drain you, taking you off track and leaving you wondering why you're not where you wanted to be.

As you go through this book, you'll find yourself becoming more aware of your current decisions and the habits that result from them. Again, that can be confronting, but only once you're aware of the choices you're making can you decide whether they align with what you truly desire.

If so, you'll learn in this section how to transform them into habits that you can do again and again without having to consciously choose each time. If you discover that your past decisions no longer serve you, you can let go of the unhelpful habits you've developed and make new choices instead.

As an example, you probably don't need to consciously use your precious energy every day to decide if you should brush your teeth or get dressed in the morning. That's because, for most of us, these are habits that we just don't think about.

However, if for some reason, you *didn't* brush your teeth for a few days in a row, you might find yourself quickly losing the habit. Suddenly, you'd have to consciously think about doing it... and you might end up developing a new habit of ignoring your teeth. The same is true of getting changed out of whatever clothes you slept in.

And if you're someone who doesn't do either of these things as a daily habit right now, you could use the awareness you gain as you read this section to explore the habits you have instead. Is what you're doing now supporting you in manifesting your desires? If not, what could support you more?

Supportive habits can transform your life

Adopting supportive habits can create an entirely new way of experiencing life.

These habits can create a kind of forward momentum that helps you to finally make and sustain the changes you desire. Once you start routinely living these habits, they naturally, inexorably move you in the direction you want to head in.

Not only that, but regularly, consistently completing an action you want to make habitual generates confidence and belief in yourself. Believing in yourself can then become its own habit.

When you believe in yourself, you say yes to more opportunities. Saying yes then *also* becomes a habit, which creates more confidence, movement and growth. And so the forward momentum continues.

Of course, the opposite is also possible. If you repeatedly choose not to take action on the habits you want to build, you'll probably feel guilty or like you've failed. Over time, you start to internalise that failure and guilt. You start to believe that you just *can't* build good habits, and that there's no point in even trying anything new.

Over the next few chapters, I want to share with you a variety of supportive magickal habits, so you can pick the ones that appeal most to you. Perhaps even more importantly, you can pick the ones you'll actually do.

Little by little, these will help you to build the momentum you need to step into the Magick of You.

Your habits don't have to be huge

Some of the habits we'll talk about in this section may seem so small that they couldn't possibly make a difference in your life. Especially at the beginning of setting up a habit, though, the fact that you're doing anything at all is often more important than the specifics of what you're doing.

Adding something onto an existing habit is always easier than creating something completely new. As James Clear, author of *Atomic Habits*, puts it:

> *"Master the habit of showing up. A habit must be established before it can be improved."*

That's why, when you're first starting out, you need to focus on simply showing up for yourself and your magick. A smaller habit might even be better. The smaller something is, the more likely you are to actually do it.

For example, let's say you want to feel more energetic during the day. Drinking a glass of water each day may seem like a small action, but it's attainable.

Running five miles every day, on the other hand, may seem admirable, and perhaps like it would create more progress towards your goal. But even just the idea of it can seem overwhelming.

Even if you don't currently drink anything but soft drinks, having a single glass of water is easy so you're likely to do it. Plus, if you forget about that glass and only remember it just before you go to bed, you can still squeeze in your daily drink of water.

And once you've established the habit, you can add something more onto it. So drinking your glass of water every day adds the momentum of achievement to your day.

By contrast, that five-mile run requires far, far more commitment and time. If you're not running at all right now, you might not be able to manage it without injuring yourself. Even if you do manage it, it's likely to leave you sore. Then, as soon as you miss your first daily run, it starts you on the slippery slope to giving up.

One missed run quickly becomes two, which then becomes:

- 'Oh, I'll start again next week'

- 'I'll wait for the weather to improve', or

- 'I'll start again when my new gear arrives'

Eventually, you realise that somehow, a couple of months have passed since you last went for a run.

It's important to note that not sticking to a habit doesn't make you a bad person. Much like with motivation, you can outgrow a habit that used to be right for you. Or sometimes, you might actively try to develop a habit that isn't right or sustainable for you.

But there's a difference between outgrowing a habit or consciously choosing to let go of it, and never giving it the chance to develop in the first place. Trying to do too much too fast is likely to result in the latter, while starting small allows your habit to bloom.

For example, let's say you want to learn to play the guitar. After doing some research, you discover that a professional musician you deeply respect practises for two hours every single day. So, since you long to become as good as she is, you decide that you too will practise for two hours each day.

How long do you think you'll be able to maintain that two-hour-a-day habit? Odds are good that it won't last long. You've probably got far too much going on in your life to put that much time aside every day.

But what if, instead of aiming to practise for two hours each day, you instead tried practising for fifteen minutes, three times a week? That's probably a lot more manageable.

After a month, you might have progressed less than if you'd actually maintained a two-hour-daily practice habit over that time... but you'll still be further ahead than if you'd done three days of two-hour sessions and then given up.

What makes a habit magickal?

When you decide to repeatedly do something that supports you in reclaiming the Magick of You, you create a magickal habit.

You're not choosing to do this thing because you think you should, or because someone else told you it would achieve a goal. You're choosing it because you know at a deep level that it aligns with the energy of the person you want to become, and supports you in manifesting your desire.

Like everything else I talk about in this book, magickal habits aren't quick fixes. Yes, sometimes they can create fast results. More often, though, they're a commitment to yourself and an investment in the future you want to create.

Building magickal habits also often isn't the easy option. Following someone else's rules may seem easier in the short term. But taking the time to get clear on what you need –

and what will work in your unique situation – is much more likely to create sustainable change.

And that, in turn, is more likely to create the results you desire.

Additionally, magickal habits bring more meaning to your day. Your new, consciously chosen habits connect you with your inner power and ability to create change, no matter how small, to steer your life in the direction of your own choosing.

Magickal habits can create a support system that honours your own sacred rhythm throughout your day. So much of your life can be governed by other people's timing and needs, which can then knock you out of your own rhythm.

You can fall into the trap of comparing yourself with others. You can try to do what they do, thinking it will give you the same results. (Spoiler alert: it won't, and we'll talk about why later in this chapter.)

Magickal habits also give you a moment to consider and connect with your own timings and needs. In a world immersed in other people's online highlight reels, your habits can help you to focus on not just the outcome you desire, but the essential process of getting there too.

Finally, magickal habits connect you with your own rhythm and flow through life. No more forcing or hustling.

Instead, they encourage you to believe in yourself and trust yourself deeply. They help you to cultivate a strong sense of connection and inner peace as you stop trying to be someone you're not and remember who you really are.

Who do you need to become?

Back in *Section 2: Your Magickal Life Philosophy*, we talked about creating a Magickal Life Philosophy. Then, over *Section 3: Your Magickal Mindset*, we explored how the right mindset can help you to live that philosophy. But another way to embody your Magickal Life Philosophy is to ask yourself who you need to become to truly live it.

In *Chapter 2.3 – Stop Apologising for Who You Are*, we looked at the importance of words and names. Now let's take this one step deeper and look at identity.

Who do you need to become to achieve your desire?
And what do you need to do to become that person?
What magickal habits do you need to create to support your becoming?

I want you to focus on 'becoming' that person, rather than 'being' them.

'Being' is a static snapshot of where you are in time. If there's too much distance between where you are now and where you want to be, bridging it can feel overwhelming, and even impossible.

'Becoming', on the other hand, is fluid. It implies movement. You can use the momentum of becoming to shift you a little in the right direction from wherever you are now.

It's perfectly OK to not quite be who you're becoming yet.

Each time you take an action towards a habit, it's like a vote for the person you're becoming. If the habit was a supportive one you chose consciously, you voted for the person you want to become. If not, it was a vote in the other direction.

Habits reinforce the person you believe yourself to be. They provide you with evidence about what you value. The more evidence you have, the more action you take in line with those values and beliefs, creating a virtuous cycle (the opposite of a vicious cycle).

Habits can help you to achieve a particular goal, but they're bigger than that. They're a way of life that allows you to fully express the Magick of You.

Activity: Exploring who you need to become

To get you started on thinking about who you need to become to live your Magickal Life Philosophy, open your journal and explore your responses to these prompts:

- How would you describe yourself as a person?

- When you think about your goals and desires for yourself, what characteristics does someone who already enjoys those things have?

- What do you need to stop doing to become more like that person?

- What do you need to start doing to become more like that person?

- What else would you need to change to become more like that person?

Building habits requires a system

Focusing on a desire is easy. Imagining having it is light and fun. It's full of hope and potential. Building the systems to get what you desire is more challenging. It requires your commitment, time, attention and resources.

Knowing what you desire is a great way to focus your energy and align yourself with what's truly important to you. It's like standing on the bank of a river you want to cross and looking at the opposite side, imagining how wonderful life will be when you get there. You can keep looking as long as you want... but until you actually start physically moving towards that other bank, nothing changes.

A system of magickal habits is like a set of stepping stones that you can use to make your crossing easier. It won't miraculously transport you to the other side. You'll still have to put one foot in front of the other to move from where you are now to where you want to be. The stepping stones just make the crossing faster and less difficult.

The more you prioritise the magickal habits in your system, the sooner you'll reach the other side of the river. Then, when you get there, not only will you be closer to the results you desire, but you'll have enjoyed the journey more too.

Make your system work for YOU

When it comes to creating a system of magickal habits, we're all individuals. The right system for you will depend on:

- your circumstances
- your access to resources
- your support system
- the way that you naturally navigate the world

And all of these factors are equally important.

There's a popular meme that shows a picture of Beyoncé with text that reads 'We all have the same 24 hours in the day'.

That's technically true... but it's also grossly misleading.

We might all have 24 hours in our days, but we don't all have the same quality of time in that 24 hours. Very few people have access to the same help, support and resources that Beyoncé has.

In our guitar learning example earlier, you probably don't have the same quality of time in your 24 hours as the professional musician who inspired you does. You might need to work a 9-5 job, while practising and performing music *is* their job.

Perhaps you also have children or other commitments in your life that they don't. And maybe the money they earn for performing allows them to outsource a lot of the domestic work that places demands on your time.

I think the Beyoncé meme is supposed to be inspiring. Unfortunately though, 'inspiration' like this can actually be disempowering. If you expect to achieve your desires in the same way that someone else does, falling short can make you feel like a failure, or at least a little defeated. No doubt you could achieve far more with access to even a small fraction of Beyoncé's resources.

However, this doesn't mean that you can't make the most of whatever your situation is. It doesn't mean you can't go for your desires and achieve them. It just means that to do it, you'll need to experiment and discover what works for you. It also means not comparing yourself or your desired outcome to someone else who already appears to have what you want.

You don't know how someone else was supported in getting to where they are now. Nor can you know their why for getting there. Even if you seem to want the same thing as them on the surface, their situation and reasons may be very different from yours.

You're each separate people with your own unique skills, magick and experiences in life.

Your superpower is being you.

Your magick is yours.

These are your gifts, so don't betray them by trying to fit into someone else's idea of success.

One size doesn't fit all

I can't stress enough how important it is that the magickal habits you decide to build reflect and align with your own desires.

They don't have to be about learning how to be more productive so that you can achieve more of what the world tells you is important. Nor do they have to be based on living some unrealistic version of wellness that isn't healthy for you.

There is no one-size-fits-all. How could there be?

Everyone has their own starting point, their own needs and desires. So the habits you choose for your system of stepping stones must reflect your authentic reality, not someone else's.

Additionally, magickal habits evolve and emerge as you do. As you embody more of your magick and rediscover what lights you up, you'll identify new habits to support you in becoming the person you want to be.

When you focus on creating everyday magickal habits that are simple, fun and doable, your progress becomes more achievable and sustainable.

Your magickal habits shift you from simply wishing that your life was different to creating a system of practices that move you towards what you desire. They support you to create real change that's aligned for you, so you can start living a life of magick, meaning and momentum.

They honour who you are and how you want to show up in the world.

As a result, your system isn't about being rigid and forcing yourself to do something in a certain way and at a certain time. Instead, it's about finding your own rhythm and flow, and what works best for you.

Activity: Exploring your current habits

We'll talk about reviewing your existing habits in more depth in the next chapter.

In the meantime, start to think about the habits you've already built and how they support or undermine your Magickal Life Philosophy.

Then take out your journal again and answer these prompts:

- What habits do you already do successfully?

- What habits do you wish you did more of, or more consistently?

- What habits do you want to implement, but end up consistently not starting or giving up on?

- How aligned is each of these habits with your Magickal Life Philosophy?

- Can you do anything to tweak the habits that aren't aligned to make them more supportive? Or is it time to put them on hold, or stop trying to force yourself to do them altogether?

Everything gets easier with practice

In *Chapter 3.2 – The Motivated MIND Mindset*, we explored all the reasons that something can be difficult without being wrong.

That's not how many people see it though. In fact, when people work with me, I often ask them what three feelings they want more of in their lives. A huge percentage of their responses include 'a feeling of ease'.

That's fair enough. I mean who wouldn't want more ease in their life?

But things *get* easy when you practise them more.

It's just like with our example of learning guitar. The first time you pick the guitar up, you probably won't know how to hold it. You may feel like you're all 'fingers and thumbs'. Perhaps you get frustrated when you know something doesn't sound right, but you're not sure how to fix it.

After a while, however, as you continue to practise, it gets easier to play. Your fingers just intuitively know where they should be. And when you make a mistake, you know what to do to get the sound back on track.

You go from focusing incredibly hard on where each finger has to be and how hard you need to press it on the string, to barely thinking about it at all. That progress happens because you keep showing up to do your practice.

In the same way, any goal you want to achieve requires you to show up and work towards it. The more often you do it, the easier it becomes.

There's no magic trick to this. People who make things look easy have generally spent a great deal of time, energy and effort on showing up and practising it over and over again.

They've probably felt like giving up many times along the way.

Perhaps they've even quit, only to choose to show up again and keep going.

As another example, if you wanted to make running a marathon easier, you'd need to put in a huge amount of training and discipline before the event. Not only would you need to build up your running stamina, but you'd also need to practise your running technique and follow smart rest, nutrition and recovery strategies.

Even then, race day might not be easy. But showing up and practising beforehand will certainly make it far easier than not practising would have done.

Yes, all that practice might seem boring, and perhaps even arduous. Who wants to repeatedly get up early to run before work, or go running in the rain? It's much more fun to visualise finishing the race, and perhaps even winning it.

However, it's the habits you create as you're showing up to practice that allow you to find your own rhythm.

They're what *create* more ease.

Building magickal habits isn't about living, laughing and loving your way through life. It's about bringing real change into reality and reminding you that the magick to create that change lies within you.

So no more looking outside of yourself for the answers. No more trying to find your motivation from external sources, unless they're the ones you feel authentically guided towards. No more comparing yourself to others.

Instead, you'll fill yourself up from the inside, and continue to develop your habits from a place of power, intentionality and alignment.

What if the habits still feel too hard or boring?

Magickal habits shouldn't be boring. By definition, they should be magickal!

If you start small the way I've recommended, they shouldn't be overly hard either. If something still feels too difficult, perhaps see if you can make it even smaller.

If you're struggling to meditate for ten minutes a day, see if you can manage five to start with. If you're struggling to run for 30 minutes three times a week, try three sessions of walking for ten minutes instead.

Remember that creating the foundation is the most important thing: you can always build on it by increasing your time or intensity later.

But what if it's not the habit's size that makes it impossible to build? What if making time to do it at all is a challenge?

If you find yourself thinking, "I just don't have enough time for this," ask yourself if that's really true. Do you genuinely not have time? If so, then maybe this isn't the right habit for you at the moment. What other habit could you focus on instead that would support your desire and move you forward towards it?

But you may find, if you're honest with yourself, that you struggle because you don't yet have the skills to prioritise the things that support you. If so, I recommend going back to the boundary-strengthening activity in *Chapter 3.3 – The Intentional MIND Mindset*. Look at where you could bolster your boundaries to cultivate the habit you want to build.

Building magickal habits is a spiral process

If you've read any self-help book, you'll already know that you're a powerful creator who can manifest a life of magick and meaning. The self-help industry tells you that you're responsible for everything you create: the good and the bad, the wanted and the unwanted.

So if you don't have what you want right now, it must in some way be your own fault.

But the idea that you're responsible for what you create is a dangerous half-truth – one that does a lot of damage.

Yes, you ARE a powerful creator.

You DO have the potential to be, do and have everything your heart desires.

But, at the same time, it's OK if you're not there yet.

And if something bad happens along the way, it's not automatically because you did something wrong. See the section on feeling guilty about negative thoughts in *Chapter 3.6 – Magickal MIND Mindset Compromisers* for more about why this belief is so toxic.

So many of my clients come to me feeling disillusioned. They'd done all the things they'd been told they needed to do to attract their ideal soul mate, manifest their dream home, build their six-figure business, etc.

They'd said their affirmations. They'd created vision boards. They'd done everything they could to stay 'high-vibe', but they still hadn't got the results they desired.

What they didn't realise is that building the habits that move them closer to the life they desire isn't a linear, one-and-done thing.

It's a multi-step process that they need to repeatedly cycle through to achieve their desires. This process involves reviewing where they are now, deciding what to change and then setting up a structure and a schedule for that change.

And then, once they've spent some time with their new habits, it involves going back to the beginning to review it all again.

As we discovered earlier, habits that worked perfectly for you previously won't necessarily work for you now. In the same way, habits that work for you now won't necessarily work for you a month, or a year, down the track.

So following this spiral process supports you in ensuring that the system of habits you build remains magickal until they generate the results you dream of.

In the rest of this section, we'll talk through the spiral process in detail, and I'll introduce you to a few of my favourite habits and systems to explore.

Key insights to take with you

- Philosophy and mindset are both important, but to make real, lasting changes in your life, you need to add in magickal everyday habits.

- Your habits don't need to be big, but they do need to be regular, and they need to be things that are doable for you.

- Much like motivation, what's doable varies from person to person – there's no 'one size fits all' when it comes to habits.

- Building magickal habits is a multi-step process that you'll cycle through over and over again in your journey towards reclaiming your magick.

A question to think about

> When have you struggled to maintain habits in the past? What could you have done to make those habits more magickal?

4.2 Review Your Existing Habits

Why you need to review

Have you ever had a friend who insisted on going on a diet because they couldn't fit into their favourite pair of jeans? Perhaps you've even succumbed to pressure and done something similar yourself?

This is something that always makes me sad because your clothes are inanimate objects that should fit *you*. You shouldn't have to alter yourself to squeeze into them!

And magickal habits are exactly the same. They should fit your life. You shouldn't have to fundamentally change who you are to make your habits fit you, no matter how good you think they might be for you.

In the last chapter, I described habits as 'the decisions we no longer have to make'.

Not having to check in with every single decision we make each day can be useful. It frees up time and mental energy to focus on other areas of our lives. It also helps us to avoid decision fatigue.

The problem is that it's easy to get caught up in being busy. Many of us are so busy doing, doing, doing that we forget to ever check in on our habits. And every so often, we need to make the time to review our habits to make sure they still work for us.

That's why the first step to setting magickal habits is to take a step back and review what you're doing right now. Evaluate what still works and is aligned for you, and keep doing those things. But also give yourself permission to stop, or at least refine, the habits that no longer serve you.

Once you take that step back, you'll start to notice clear signs if a habit needs reviewing. Perhaps you realise you've been doing it less often. Maybe you've stopped doing it altogether. Perhaps it's started to feel like a burden that takes more from you than it gives. Or maybe you simply realise that you've only been doing it for the sake of doing it.

If you notice any of these signs, there's a good chance that something about that habit needs to change.

For example, with a gratitude journal, think about how you feel when you fill it out. It's much more effective to really feel and connect with your gratitude, rather than just mindlessly listing out items to go through the motions of getting it done.

So for each habit you've been working on bringing into your life, ask yourself:

- Does it still support the decisions you've made about what you want in your life now?

- Is it still moving you forward towards your desire?

- Or have you started doing it just for the sake of doing it?

Don't confuse action with momentum

When you're busy, it can feel like you're getting a lot done. But one downside of constant busy-ness is assuming that getting a lot done automatically means you're making progress.

Of course, taking action is important. Just make sure your actions are genuinely moving you in the right direction. Much like with the car we mentioned in the Introduction, if you travel in a random direction, you won't necessarily end up closer to your goal. You might just end up driving around in circles, or maybe even moving further away from where you want to be.

Similarly, as you review your habits, don't confuse simply doing things with creating momentum.

Shopping for new gym gear isn't the same as actually working out. Yes, if your goal is to feel healthier and more energetic, it's a step in the right direction (assuming you actually needed new gym gear). It only takes you so far, though, and it may even be a distraction.

In the same way, signing up for a gym membership and stopping there doesn't improve your fitness. You still need to show up at the gym and then *work out* to make any progress.

So as you're reviewing the actions you've been taking, ask yourself:

- What choices have you repeatedly made?
- What actions have you repeatedly taken?
- How have those actions moved you forward towards your desires?

Remember that your choices inform your behaviours. Your behaviours become your habits. And it's your habits that move you towards achieving your intentions and desires.

Once again, if you discover that your choices haven't really moved you forward, don't blame yourself or make yourself wrong. Just make a note that the habit is one you'll need to look at either replacing or refining.

We'll talk more about what you might want to replace or refine it *with* in the next chapter.

Or, if you still feel like the habit would serve you but you're just not doing it as often as you want to, it may help to revisit your mindset. Try going back and re-reading *Section 3: Your Magickal Mindset* before recommitting to the habit again.

Then move on to your next habit, and evaluate that too.

Keep going until you've looked at all of the habits that relate to your desire.

Refining your energetic influences

As you review your habits, be aware that you need to pay attention to more than just the physical effects of your choices. It's also important to review how your habits impact your energy.

What you consume becomes part of you. It becomes part of your energy.

This is important, because it's easy to see how your choices affect your physical progress towards your desires. Their effect on your energy, however, can be more subtle. You may not even notice that your choices have had an effect... until suddenly, you find yourself feeling overwhelmed, frustrated or burnt out.

And once more, it's a cycle. Your choices affect your energy, which in turn affects your ability to make supportive choices in the future. When your energy feels depleted, it's so much harder to make the choices that create your magickal habits and allow you to fully reclaim and embody your magick.

If the energy you surround yourself with supports your energy system and aligns with your truth, it helps you to align with the Magick of You. If that energy disempowers you, it will dull your connection with yourself and your magick. You'll find it harder to connect with and trust yourself and the messages you receive from your soul.

So what are the most significant elements of the choices that influence your energy? They're the things that you energetically consume each day. I've called them 'energetic influences' in the activity that follows.

As we talked about in _Chapter 1.3 – Understanding Energy_, everything in life is an exchange of energy. Do your habits create energetic influences that nourish and support you? Or do those influences distract and deplete you?

Rate the following aspects of the energetic influences in your life on a scale of 0 to 10, where:

- 0 means you feel awful, disconnected from your truth, and full of fear and judgement in this area.
- 10 means this area totally aligns with your highest good, keeping you fully connected to your intuition and confidently acting on your inspirations.

Physical basics

These include your food, drink and sleep, as well as fresh air and movement.

Ask yourself:

- Do you mostly eat foods that nourish you or foods that your intuition knows don't support you?
- How much sleep do you get? Is it enough, or do you regularly feel physically tired?
- Do you get out of the house and breathe fresh air (or at least open the windows), or do you only breathe stale or recycled air?
- How often do you move your body? Is movement a joy, or does it feel like a chore?

Give yourself a rating out of 10 for this area.

Environmental health

This includes the things you surround yourself with in the places you spend the most time, for example, your home, workspace or car.

Ask yourself:

- Are you surrounded by things that add to your quality of life?
- Does your environment flow or is it full of clutter?
- Do you enjoy being in these environments?
- Do your environments support the purpose they're designed for? For example, do you feel rested in your bedroom, nourished in your kitchen and productive at work?

Give yourself a rating out of 10 for this area.

Emotional health

This includes your connections with friends and family, your emotions and your feelings.

Ask yourself:

- Are you in relationships with reliable people that you can trust to look out for your highest good, or do you have to 'manage' yourself and the relationship?
- Do you feel a deep sense of connection in your relationships, or are they superficial?
- Is it easy for you to express your emotions, or do you find yourself holding them in?
- Do you trust your feelings, or do you feel safer only using reason and logic to navigate the world?

Give yourself a rating out of 10 for this area.

Information balance

This includes the information you take in through books, newspapers and magazines, education and learning, TV, movies and social media.

Ask yourself:

- Do the books, newspapers and magazines you read raise your vibration and make you feel hopeful and joyful, or do they leave you feeling hopeless?
- Do you allow yourself to learn new things and follow your curiosity, or do you need a specific reason to learn something new?
- Do the social media pages or channels you follow uplift, inform or inspire you, or do they leave you feeling that you and your life aren't good enough?
- How do you feel after you finish the majority of movies and TV shows you watch?

Give yourself a rating out of 10 for this area.

Spiritual health

This includes your connection to your 'something bigger', as well as your use of sacred ritual, meditation and prayer.

Ask yourself:

- Do you have a deep trust in something bigger than yourself, or do you try to control outcomes and other people?
- Do you perform any sacred rituals to bring you a sense of spiritual connection in your life?

- Do you have a regular meditation practice that clears your mind and helps you to find some inner peace and calm?

- Do you have a prayer practice, or a practice where you connect with or talk to your 'something bigger'?

Give yourself a rating out of 10 for this area.

Energetic health

This includes your own spiritual or journaling practices and could include your use of essential oils, herbs and crystals. It could also include simply spending time in nature.

Ask yourself:

- Do you regularly prioritise your energetic health, or is it something you leave for 'when you have enough time' or during emergencies?

- Do you have a journaling practice that helps you to release all that's on your mind?

- Do you work with allies such as essential oils, herbs and crystals to support your energy system?

- Do you make time to be in nature so you can balance your energy and feel grounded?

Give yourself a rating out of 10 for this area.

What changes do you need to make?

Finally, once you've rated yourself in each of these areas, it's time to decide what you want to do with this information. For any area where your rating was lower than you'd like, ask yourself:

- What habits prevent or distract you from embodying the Magick of You?

- What habits would support you in accessing and trusting the Magick of You?

- What do you need to stop or start doing to help you more easily access the Magick of You?

- What do you need to nourish and continue doing to keep embodying the Magick of You?

Use the answers to these questions to help you prioritise where you need to focus your magickal habits. What changes in your daily life will support your energetic health and connect you to your intuition, creativity and magick?

These will be vital pieces of information to help you create magickal habits that truly benefit you.

If you want to refine or replace multiple habits...

If you discover lots of areas that need improvement, just focus on one to start with. Trying to address all of them at once is a surefire recipe for overwhelm and inaction. You can always choose a new area to focus on once you're comfortable with your changes in the first one.

Or you could choose a new area each month, or even each week.

But whatever habit you focus on, make sure you're doing it regularly – if not daily – before you shift your focus to something else. Much like with going to the gym to work out, yes, taking action towards your habit sporadically is better than not doing it at all...

But leave it too long since you last did something, and you'll lose most of your momentum – in the same way you'd lose the benefits you'd gained from your last workout.

As a result, you'll constantly be starting again from zero.

Prioritising the habits that support your energy a little more frequently enables you to keep building on your previous progress. So, over time, you'll build up the stamina, resilience and strength that deepens your connection with the Magick of You.

Key insights to take with you

- It's important to review your habits regularly to ensure they're still working for you, rather than believing that you need to change yourself to fit your habits.

- Don't assume that just because you're taking action, you must be moving forward: not everything you do will create momentum.

- Check the effects of your habits on your energy as well as your physical progress – if your energy's depleted, it's hard to make the choices that become supportive habits.

- Once you've identified the habits that aren't working for you, ask yourself whether you want to refine them or replace them altogether.

A question to think about

Which habits do you already know you need to refine or replace? Which do you need to explore more before you make a decision?

4.3 Soul Vitamin Habits

Why 'soul vitamins'?

When you have a big desire, some habits create a foundation of daily actions that directly help to get you there. For example, if you want to write a book, the habit of writing a certain number of words each day (or each week) directly helps to get you there. If you want to travel, saving a certain amount of money each week directly helps to get you there.

But other habits are smaller. They support you in moving closer to your desires less directly. Often, they help by improving the quality of your energy. As we talked about in the previous chapter, when your energy is aligned with your desires, it becomes so much easier to make the choices that directly support you in achieving them.

So in this chapter, I want to introduce you to some of these smaller habits, which I call 'soul vitamins'.

Soul vitamins are the small habits that you do regularly, often daily, to create the perfect foundation for you to live the Magick of You and embrace the life you desire. Much like vitamins nourish your body and maintain a foundation of health, soul vitamin habits help to create a healthy, nourishing environment for your desires.

Vitamins only work as long as you keep taking them

Soul vitamins work in the same kind of way as multivitamins do too.

The first time you take a multivitamin, you probably won't notice any difference in how you feel. After a few weeks, though, you may discover that you feel more alert. Perhaps you have more energy, or you're sleeping better.

You'll probably continue to enjoy the effects as long as you keep taking it regularly. It's the cumulative effect of taking a multivitamin over time that benefits you, not individual one-off tablets.

However, as time goes by, you might start to forget what life was like before your well-being improved. Your newfound energy levels and alertness are just normal now. So you start to wonder why you're even taking the multivitamin when you no longer seem to need it.

Perhaps you start taking it less regularly. Maybe you even stop taking it altogether. Then, slowly but surely, you start to feel a little less vibrant. Your sleep becomes more disturbed again. You begin to tire more quickly.

Until, without even noticing, you've returned to the old level of health that you'd originally started taking your multivitamin to change.

The same is true with your soul vitamins.

The first time you do one of the 'soul vitamin' habits, you probably won't notice any immediate change. Over time, though, you'll find you feel more resilient, bolder and able to believe more deeply in yourself.

Not only will you *feel* better, but you'll also notice yourself making more of the decisions that directly support you in achieving your desires. You'll find it gets easier to choose the actions that reconnect you with yourself and your magick.

And just as with multivitamins, when you stop doing these habits, you once again – slowly but surely – drift further away from the Magick of You.

Specific soul vitamin habits

So what exactly *are* soul vitamins? They're practices I've alluded to in previous chapters, such as:

- affirmations
- mirror work
- journaling
- gratitude practices
- visualisation
- meditation
- nature walks

I'll talk about each of these in more depth shortly.

In the meantime, what's important is to recognise that each time you do one of these practices, it nourishes your dreams and desires. It helps you to reconnect with what's important to you. It gives your soul the necessary nutrients to create change, move forward and enjoy a more magickal life.

I'm sure you've already heard of most of these practices. If you've ever read any self-help book before, you'll know they get recommended over and over again. That's because they're important and they work, at least when you do them effectively.

You may have experience in doing some of these practices yourself. A few may already be components of your current spiritual, energetic or self-care practices. However, if they are, it's worth reviewing them as we discussed in the previous chapter.

How supportive do they feel the way that you're currently doing them?

Are they energising you and leaving you feeling more nourished?

If so, by all means, keep doing them the way that you're doing them now. If not, it's worth checking whether you're just going through the motions with them.

In the rest of this chapter, I want to share a slightly different take on each of these practices to help you get the most out of them.

Let's start with affirmations.

Affirmations

Affirmations are simple statements you repeat regularly that describe an outcome or a desire – something you want to be, do or have.

Done right, they can be a powerful way to change your negative self-talk into something more positive and supportive. They can give your soul the stamina to move in the direction of the relationship you want to create with yourself and the world around you.

However, whilst affirmations are very popular, many people actually create terrible affirmations that do nothing to support them. Done wrong, these affirmations can even have the opposite effect to what the people saying them desire.

Affirmation basics

You can use any wording you like for an affirmation, and it can affirm any desire or outcome you want to bring into reality. You can use other people's wording if it particularly resonates for you, or create your own if you feel drawn to.

Whatever you say, I recommend sticking to three basic rules:

- **Phrase the affirmation positively**. Describe what you *do* want, not what you don't. Say, "I love and accept myself," rather than, "I've stopped hating myself". If you find it hard to identify the positive thing you want, ask yourself what it would feel like to no longer do the thing you don't want. Use that in your affirmation instead.

- **Phrase it in the present tense**. Describe the outcome as though it's already happening. Say, "I love and accept myself," rather than, "I want to love and accept myself".

- **Make it believable for you right now**. If your mind immediately sneers, "Yeah right, whatever, who are you kidding?" you're just affirming the dismissal. Try to find a baby step on the way to your outcome that you can believe in. Say, "I am open to loving and accepting myself," instead of, "I completely love and accept myself".

Belief is essential

The third point in the list above is particularly important. The traditional approach to affirmations is to focus on your end goal. So you might learn to say classic affirmations like:

- 'I love and accept myself completely.'

- 'I am perfect just as I am.'

- 'I believe in myself unwaveringly.'

But if you don't love and accept yourself completely right now, simply saying it doesn't make it true. If you know full well that you DON'T consider yourself perfect right now, or that your belief in yourself regularly wavers, just stating the opposite won't change things.

Instead, your mind will tell you whatever you truly believe right now as a counter to the affirmation. It will come up with evidence for why the affirmation isn't true. Let's take 'I'm perfect just as I am' from above. If you say this while knowing that you don't believe it, your mind's immediate response will probably be something like:

- "No, you're not: you yelled at your daughter yesterday when she acted out!"

- "You? Perfect? When you haven't worked out in five days now? I don't think so."

- "Nuh-uh. Perfect people recycle and compost and live zero-waste lifestyles. That's not you."

So each time you repeat the affirmation, your mind immediately gives you the counter... and that's what you end up affirming.

Making affirmations magickal

Finding a more realistic baby step to affirm – something on the path to your end goal, but which doesn't strain your belief now – avoids this issue. That's why, instead of affirming where you want to be, I recommend acknowledging where you are and then creating the possibility of change.

So instead of saying 'I love myself', try something like:

- 'I'm open to loving myself.'
- 'Each day it becomes easier to love myself.'
- 'I love myself more every day.'
- 'Every day I learn more ways to love myself.'
- 'I'm starting to understand why I'm loveable.'

Now, when you say your affirmation, your mind isn't judging whether or not the end goal is true. It's only judging whether the affirmation could be possible in future. You're opening the door of possibility, which is much easier for your subconscious or inner critic to get on board with.

Notice how you feel when you say the phrases out loud:

- 'I love myself.'
- 'I am open to loving myself.'

Which gave you a feeling of expansion? Which, if any, contracted your energy?

I hope the first one created that expansion for you. If it didn't, start where you are now. Instead of spending all of your precious energy trying to convince yourself that you're something you know you aren't yet, accept where you are. Then start moving forward in a new direction, taking your subconscious mind and inner critic along with you, but in their calm state.

Hopefully, that feels much better. If so, let's continue to improve it.

Incorporating action

We've explored the cycle of actions creating your beliefs and beliefs feeding your actions in earlier sections. You can use this concept in your affirmations too.

You can *make* your affirmations truer by adding an action to them.

'I love myself more each day' can become 'I love myself more each day, and today I show it by...' Then add an action on the end – something that you can do to show yourself love.

Once again, choose a small action that you'll actually do. This is much more powerful than choosing something bigger that you might only manage to do occasionally.

In the example above, you might show yourself love by:

- drinking more water
- stretching and moving your body
- going to bed before midnight
- saying yes to an opportunity
- saying no to an invitation

You can choose a different action each day, or even each time you say the affirmation (once you've done whatever you've said you'd do the last time).

Whatever you choose, make it something you can tangibly do. That way, not only are you changing your thought patterns, but you're also backing up the belief you want to create with action that supports it.

When, where and how

Finally, to really get the most out of your affirmations, you need to say them out loud regularly. The more often you say them, the more you feel them and the more powerful they become.

I recommend saying them at least once every morning, and then ideally regularly throughout your day. Feel free to get creative with them too. Try:

- repeating them in the shower

- singing them as you make your breakfast

- recording them on your phone and listening to them as you walk, run or drive

For an extra dose of magick, repeat them while looking yourself in the eye in the mirror (more about this in the next soul vitamin section on mirror work). This may be uncomfortable to start with, but the more you do it, the easier and more enjoyable the experience becomes.

And yes, it's important to say your affirmations out loud. We believe so much of the negative self-talk we hear *because* we hear it in our own voice. It may have originally come from internalising the external voices and words of people around us. But we've repeated it to ourselves so often that it now sounds like our own voice.

Hearing yourself saying the affirmations out loud – especially if you record yourself saying them and listen to the recordings – is a powerful way to counter that internalised voice. Especially if you use headphones, so the voice you hear is 'in your head', it sounds more like the self-talk you've believed up till now.

Above all though, remember that affirmations aren't just an exercise to cross off your to-do list. They're nourishment for your soul and your desires, so saying them needs to feel that way.

You're saying the words because you want to activate your magick and initiate change.

You're saying them because you want to experience more peace, power and purpose in your life.

Mirror work

I said above that saying your affirmations whilst looking at yourself in the mirror can make the affirmations more powerful. In magickal self-care circles, this is often referred to as mirror work.

The first person I ever heard talk about mirror work was Louise Hay. She said it worked because:

> *"... the mirror reflects back to you the feelings you have about yourself. It makes you immediately aware of where you are resisting and where you are open and flowing."*

You don't need to say affirmations to get this effect. Even if you just look at yourself silently, the mirror gives you immediate feedback as to how you feel about yourself.

This can be a little unnerving to start with.

In fact, if you've never done mirror work before, I'd recommend starting by just looking into the mirror silently. Gaze into your own eyes for a few breaths.

If you immediately notice your flaws and imperfections, try to breathe through the judgements. Look for the inner beauty that's shining out from the person looking back at you. Search for the magick within that person.

This isn't about comparing yourself to some external standard of beauty that's imposed by the media. It's about looking for the radiant light that shines out from your innermost being.

Whilst this practice may sound simple, it's incredibly profound. It can often bring people to tears.

Taking the time to look at yourself – to *see* yourself – is incredibly important. It helps you to connect intimately with the Magick of You.

It's OK if it's uncomfortable

As you start to look deeply into the mirror, you may feel uncomfortable. That's perfectly normal. Choose to keep showing up and practising despite the discomfort.

As you gradually get more comfortable with the process, start saying your affirmation/s while maintaining eye contact with yourself in the mirror.

Look yourself in the eye and tell yourself that you love yourself. Let yourself know that you're open to loving yourself more and more each day. Talk to yourself deeply with love, kindness, and compassion. Tell yourself all the things you've wanted other people to tell you over the years.

Take your time. Don't rush it. Just be with yourself.

Celebrate with a high-five

After you've looked yourself in the eye and said your affirmation to the you in the mirror, I want you to high-five that you.

Yes, really. After all, who do you high-five and why?

You high-five friends and people you care about to support them or recognise that they've done something well.

So, high-five yourself. Let yourself know that you support yourself, and that you're doing a great job. Even if you don't consciously feel that you are, the high-five and its positive associations reinforce the message.

Then, after the high-five, give yourself a cheeky wink in the mirror.

Once again, yes, really.

Again, you wink at people you like and trust – people who are on your side. A wink is like a secret communication that only you and that person share. It tells them they're safe with you.

So winking at yourself in the mirror is another way to affirm that you're on your own side.
Also, hopefully, the cheeky wink will make you smile.
And that's important too: it reminds you that the work of changing your life is deep and profound, but it doesn't have to be heavy.

Finally, as you go through your day, give yourself another cheeky wink whenever you see your reflection.

This will not only lift your energy and make you smile. It will give you a moment to pause and connect with yourself deeply, too.

Journaling

There are many different ways to journal and many benefits attributed to journaling. Some of those benefits include helping you to:

- fully reflect on situations you've experienced

- explore your feelings about those situations

- release tension and stored emotions

- create clarity in areas that confuse you

- identify self-talk and other patterns (both positive and negative).

Beyond these psychological benefits, journaling can also be a fun way to record your experiences, track your goals and record your growth and progress over time.

Ways to journal

There's no one right way to journal. Writing a list is a form of journaling. So is responding to journal prompts. You can also just write whatever comes to mind. It doesn't need to make sense. And some people even journal visually, for example, collaging or doodling in an art journal.

A journal session can take you a few minutes... or multiple hours if you want it to. Some people like to write several pages of pure stream-of-consciousness, but your journaling could be as simple as writing a single sentence or drawing a doodle each day.

Popular ways of journaling to reclaim and embody the Magick of You and deepen your self-awareness include:

- **art journaling** to explore your thoughts and feelings visually through art

- **dream journaling** to help you connect with the messages your dreams have for you

- **gratitude journaling** to increase the joy, pleasure and other positive feelings in your life

- **reflective journaling** to help you explore and make sense of situations, either past or present

- **Morning Pages journaling** to clear your mind of any blocks and start the day fresh each morning through stream-of-consciousness, pen-and-paper journaling

The pen-and-paper vs digital debate

Some people like to only write with a pen and paper. Others prefer, or can only use, their computer, tablet or phone. Still others do a mix of the two with different journals in different formats.

So which is better?

Writing by hand is usually slower than typing, and some people claim that slowing down forces you to become more present with yourself and your thoughts. There *might* be a bit of science behind this. For example, in 2016, Forbes said:

> *"According to a study performed at the Indiana University, the mere action of writing by hand unleashes creativity not easily accessed in any other way. And high-tech magnetic resonance imaging has indeed shown that low-tech writing by hand increases neural activity in certain sections of the brain, much like meditation."*

Additionally, in her popular Morning Pages journaling technique from her book *The Artist's Way*, Julia Cameron advocates strongly for longhand (pen-and-paper) journaling.

But... you can also become present when you're typing, especially if you consciously set the intention to type at a slower speed.

In my experience, writing by hand does help me to notice my thoughts and behaviour patterns more than when I type. However, everyone is different, and I believe that any journaling – longhand, typing or even audio or video journals – will create benefits. Much like with habits generally, the best kind of journaling is the one you'll actually do.

To find out which forms work best for you, I suggest practising with different styles and ways of journaling. Realise too that as you grow and evolve, what works for you may change over time.

SCAT pages

For the longest time, I loved to do Julia Cameron's Morning Pages. This involved writing three pages longhand about anything that came to mind. It didn't have to make sense. I was just clearing my thoughts and feelings to start my day from a centred, grounded place.

But... eventually, I just found myself writing about the same stuff over and over again. Instead of feeling like writing was helping me to clear whatever I needed to process away, I started to feel like the practice compounded it.

When I reviewed my habits the way we talked about in the last chapter, I realised that Morning Pages weren't helping me to move through anything. So I stopped doing them.

But soon, I missed having a dedicated journaling process.

When I looked at how I could refine the practice, I discovered that I needed more of a structure, but not *too* much. I thought about what I'd want to cover during a journaling session, and found myself writing four words:

- Spew/Spill
- Celebrate
- Answers
- Thoughts

And so SCAT pages were born.

Usually, I'm given acronyms like DANCE, SACRED or GRACE... but this time, I got SCAT, which I immediately associate with animal droppings. Then again, I guess the technique is a great way to get rid of what's weighing you down, so it's not inappropriate.

Activity: the SCAT pages process

I like to do my SCAT journaling before I go to bed, to bring a close to my day. But of course, do it any time that feels good for you.

If you do any other kinds of journaling, I suggest putting your SCAT pages in a separate, dedicated journal. You don't want to get SCAT over everything (haha).

I chose a black-covered notebook for mine, so it would hold and contain the energy, but you might feel drawn to something different. As always, just follow whatever feels right.

Then, once you're ready, spend as much – or as little – time as you want on each of the four steps in the acronym. Here are some ideas for each step.

Spew/Spill

This part is very similar to Morning Pages, in that you just spew/spill your thoughts and feelings over the pages. Write whatever you want, and as much or as little as you want to.

None of it has to make sense. Just let yourself write whatever you want to.

There are no rules. There's no structure. Not even any grammar if you don't want it.

Purge. Clear. Release.

If you're stuck with what to write, just start with that... 'I'm not sure what to write today, but I thought I'd start with this...'

See what words spill over the page after that.

Celebrate

Next, write a list of everything you can celebrate. This kind of judgement-free celebration does more than just make you feel good, although that's important too. It also allows you to build on your successes, helping you to achieve more of what's important to you over time.

So write a DONE-list, which is the opposite of a to-do list.

Start by celebrating all the big wins and major items you've checked off your to-do list. This might include:

- having a difficult conversation to maintain your boundaries

- completing a task you'd been postponing for months.

- getting a pay rise or a new job offer

- saying no to someone else and prioritising your own needs instead

Next, celebrate all the everyday self-care tasks that you've completed. Include things like:

- washing and other personal hygiene tasks
- ensuring you have clean clothes to wear
- grocery shopping and preparing meals so you have food to eat
- moving your body
- staying hydrated
- taking your vitamins
- arranging health appointments
- going to bed early or taking a nap

After that, celebrate completing everyday chores that maintain the home you live in. These are tasks like:

- cleaning and tidying so that your house is a comfortable place to live
- putting bins out so that your rubbish gets collected
- paying your utility (and other) bills on time

Then, celebrate crossing off any everyday tasks that keep your life running smoothly, such as:

- keeping your car fuelled up
- returning library books before they're due
- managing your money
- making sure you get to work on time
- getting your children to school on time with their homework completed

Finally, celebrate everything about yourself, and how you've shown up for yourself (and others), including times when you've:

- supported friends, family, community members or even complete strangers
- given your time or resources to others – perhaps helping a friend, or donating to charity
- offered a kind word or encouraged someone to make a change
- helped someone with a new hobby
- listened to someone who needed to talk
- given advice when someone asked you for guidance

Also celebrate times when other people have shown up for you in any of these ways.

Celebrate *everything* you've done, or that you feel grateful for and appreciate.

Celebrate. Celebrate. Celebrate.

Answers

Next, write down a question that you have, and then allow yourself to answer it.

Ask as many questions as you like, answering each one in turn.

If you don't have any pressing questions, simply ask, "What do you want me to know?"

It's important not to miss this stage, particularly if you feel you don't have any questions. You might be avoiding something, or you could be ready to go deeper.

Thoughts

This final section gives you a space to review and witness any additional thoughts that come to mind. It's a chance to process and bring clarity to anything you uncovered during your SCAT session.

So there you have it... a daily SCAT practice to keep everything 'flowing and moving' as it should do.

Gratitude and appreciation practices

A powerful way to celebrate yourself and your life exactly as they are right now, regardless of where you want to be, is through gratitude practices.

When you focus on being grateful, you're aligning yourself with the energy of being grateful, and what you're grateful for. You're attracting the vibration and energy behind the grateful feeling.

So the feeling of being grateful *can* be lovely: warm, expansive and uplifting.

Taking time to appreciate everything you're grateful for when the world feels chaotic can lift your mood and remind you of the good things you already have. Taking a moment to acknowledge everything you've done, achieved or have access to can also boost your self-esteem.

So it's not surprising that gratitude practices have become increasingly popular.

And, much like with journaling, there are many ways to include gratitude practices in your day. A practice can look like:

- writing a list of the things, activities, circumstances and people in your life that you're grateful for

- writing thank you notes to people, including yourself, that you're grateful for

- meditating on the people in your life and reflecting on how they enhance your life and how you enhance theirs

- taking a few moments to simply savour all of the good in your life and the world.

Again, experiment with different techniques to see which – if any – feel right for you.

Not all 'gratitude' works for everyone

As wonderful as gratitude can be, I stopped doing traditional 'gratitude practices' a long time ago.

Back then, the self-development world was all about being grateful. You focused on gratitude so you'd receive more to be grateful for.

That made perfect sense, and yet it felt wrong. Something about it just didn't sit right for me.

I had many, many things to be grateful for... but the idea of 'being grateful' had also always felt dense and heavy to me. The energy wasn't expansive or euphoric the way I was told it should be.

Eventually, I realised that part of it was because this kind of gratitude was positioned as the holy grail of 'fixing' what was missing in my life.

It felt similar to the way that toxic positivity required me to focus on pleasant, feel-good, high-vibes-only thoughts and ignore anything unpleasant in my life that needed to change. This kind of gratitude required me to ignore the fact that there were things I knew I wanted and didn't have, and to instead focus on all the other good things I had.

Gratitude can also be a double-edged sword

The other part of the energetic denseness and heaviness behind feeling grateful took me longer to work out. I knew I didn't feel not-grateful... and nobody wants to think of themselves as ungrateful!

Finally, I realised that gratitude was a 'should' for a large part of my childhood. When I thought about being grateful, here are the echoes that rang through my mind:

- "You should be grateful. There are people who have it much worse than you!"
- "Eat all of your dinner up. Be grateful you have food at all. People are starving in other countries."
- "Be grateful that your father isn't here. He wouldn't have let you off so lightly."

This turned gratitude into a double-edged sword. Of course, I was glad things weren't worse than they were, or that I wasn't a starving child, or that I wasn't in even more trouble. But this kind of gratitude was about a guilt trip, not a reason to be joyous.

Then, as I grew older, gratitude became tainted with the energy of struggling to overcome something. I often found myself thinking:

- "I'm so grateful that awful exam's over. Only two more to go now."
- "I'm just grateful that I didn't fall over in front of all those people and make a fool of myself."

Yes, this gratitude was still technically an expression of thanks, but it was one that felt closed and heavy. It felt like overcoming a battle.

So, whenever someone told me to keep a gratitude diary or make lists of things I was grateful for each night, my heart sank a little. Initially, I dutifully wrote them. I didn't want to appear ungrateful, after all.

But they never brought me the joy I expected them to.

Appreciation vs gratitude

One day, I realised that I didn't want to be grateful for things in my life. Instead, I wanted to appreciate them.

Now, some people might not see much difference between being grateful for something and appreciating it. For me, though, the difference was huge.

'Appreciation' felt much lighter and more joyful. It felt like a choice I made, rather than one that was forced upon me to avoid feeling ashamed or guilty.

Appreciation is the act of recognising that something is valuable or important. That, to me, felt deeper than just giving thanks. It felt more freeing and expansive.

This difference may seem like a simple thing. It may not seem that important.

But as I keep saying in this book, it's *always* important to do things your way. You need to figure out the way that's most aligned for you, even if it's completely different from how everyone else around you does something.

In other words, if you find that something isn't working for you, don't force yourself to do it that way. Don't assume you need to fix it *or* yourself.

Instead, ask yourself why it doesn't work.

Think about what that activity really means to you.

Ask how you might do it differently, in your own way, if you remembered and celebrated who you truly were.

Break it down into the individual words you're using if you have to.

In my case, I completely agreed with the concept of gratitude practices. I just needed to tweak them slightly into 'appreciation practices' that felt more spacious and aligned for me.

Activity: Doing gratitude YOUR way

Whether you prefer feeling grateful or appreciative (maybe it's both?), this practice can be magickal, especially when your day seems ordinary.

It can bring you back to your senses, allowing you to slow down and notice all the amazing things you can see, hear, touch, smell and taste. It can also help you to move through each of your senses, recalling and even re-experiencing your favourite things.

1. **First, take a few deep, centring breaths**.

2. **Then, start with what you can see.** What sights are you most grateful for? These could be shapes, colours, landscapes, movements, or even a person, plant or creature.

3. **Next, move to the world of hearing.** What are your favourite sounds? These could be words or music you enjoy. Perhaps you appreciate the rhythmic crash of ocean waves, the melodies of birdsong or the laughter of crowds.

4. **After that, move to your sense of texture and touch.** What sensations delight you? A cuddle with a person or pet? Beautiful fabric against your skin? Or maybe it's a cool breeze on your cheek on a summer morning, or the glowing warmth of a fire on a cold day.

5. **Then move to your sense of smell – one of the most evocative senses.** What scents uplift you or bring you comfort? Which bring back wonderful memories? Perhaps your favourite aromas might be flowers, a comfort food, the salt-filled seaside air, heady perfumes or old bookshops.

6. **Finally, move to your sense of taste.** What flavours and textures do you love? Which tastes make you salivate? A childhood favourite meal prepared with love? An exquisite fine-dining meal paired with a delicious wine? A hearty, comforting favourite? Do you enjoy soft, silky textures, or something with crunch? An ice-cold beverage or a piping hot one?

Allow yourself as long as you like to simply enjoy and appreciate the sensory memories of each of your favourite things. Then finish by thanking yourself for making the time to practise the energy of gratitude and appreciate all the sensations that are always available to you.

Visualisation (aka imagining)

Before we start talking about visualisation, let's dispel a myth. Despite the name, visualisation doesn't *have* to be visual. It's simply about imagining what you want as though you already have it.

Whether or not you imagine this visually, the practice can be a powerful tool to help you connect with and focus on your dreams. Focusing on what it would be like to make your desires real can help you to move towards them by:

- tapping into the sense of empowerment that manifesting them can bring
- creating positive associations with the journey of working towards your dreams, not just the destination of achieving them
- giving you ideas for creative ways to overcome any obstacles you encounter
- providing opportunities to practise or rehearse how you'll respond to various situations
- stepping you into the energy of what you want to experience.

As I said above, while this practice is usually called visualising, you don't have to focus on what you can see. Let visualisation be a full-body experience. You might be able to see clearly how life will be when you've reached your desire, but it's fine if you just see a hazy image.

Maybe it's more natural for you to *feel* what having your dream would be like, perhaps as textures on your skin, or as a sense of movement. Or maybe you can hear the conversations you'd have with friends or family in your mind's ear. You could even try to imagine the smells you'd notice.

For example, let's say your dream is to own a cosy cottage by the sea with fruit trees in its garden. To visualise this, you might imagine any or all of:

- how the cottage looks from the outside, and perhaps the colours of the wildflowers in your garden, or the view of the ocean from your kitchen window (sight)
- the kiss of the sea breezes on your skin as you stand in the garden, or maybe the cosy warmth once you've lit a fire in the hearth (touch)
- the chorus of birdsong in the garden, the crackle of the fire in the hearth or the pounding of the surf in the background as you go to bed(sound)
- the sharp scent of salt in the air, the green aroma of your garden after the rain or the tart sweetness of an apple you've grown on your tree (smell/taste)
- the physical sense of walking down the driveway, reaching out for the door handle and opening it, or drawing back the curtains in the morning (movement)

So whether you're 'a visual person' or not, it's not about picking just one sense. Instead, it's about bringing as many of your senses to the experience as you can.

1. To practice your visualising skills, simply close your eyes and imagine a place where you feel calm and rested.

   Perhaps it's somewhere that holds happy memories for you. Or maybe it's somewhere you've never been, but would love to visit.

   Either way, spend a few moments visualising that place.

2. Then, bring the visualisation to life as much as possible. Incorporate as many of your senses as you can. Ask yourself:

   - What can you see?

   - What temperature is it? Can you feel a cool mist of rain, or the warmth of the sun on your face?

   - What can you hear around you? Are people laughing? Is music playing? Can you hear the rustle of leaves in a nearby tree?

   - Notice what you can smell. Maybe there's sun lotion, the sweetness of fresh fruit or the scent of damp, mossy forests?

   - How do you feel emotionally in this place?

Get as much detail into your visualisation as possible, and allow this special place of yours to refresh and renew you.

Meditation

Meditation is the practice of focusing your attention on something specific – whether that's your breath, a word or phrase, or the feeling of walking.

Many cultures have used forms of meditation to gain a greater sense of awareness, and as a tool to enhance their focus. Meditation can also help you to:

- calm your mind

- change your mood

- reduce your stress

- increase your self-awareness

- generally become more present

Unfortunately, when people today think about meditation, they imagine having to sit cross-legged on the floor and clear their minds of all thoughts for hours. Now, if that works for you, that's great! But if it doesn't, remember there are lots of ways to meditate, so as always, find what works for you.

Meditation's calming effect can help you to connect with the Magick of You because, when you start to move towards your dreams, doubts and fears can often show up. Meditating can support your Magickal MIND mindset to help you step out of these patterns.

Forms of meditation

There are several ways you can meditate. Try a few to see which work best for you.

Focused attention

This type of meditation involves focusing on one thing, usually by sitting still and trying to ignore the distractions of everything around you. You could focus on:

- rhythmic breathing
- repeating a word or phrase
- counting something such as beads
- looking at or visualising an object

Mindful attention

This type of meditation involves becoming mindfully aware of your ordinary actions and being completely present as you do them. For example, you might bring mindfulness to:

- walking
- gardening
- a household chore like washing dishes
- any everyday activity or sequence of events

Guided attention

This type of meditation involves following spoken instructions from someone else. You'd normally listen to that person leading the meditation, either face-to-face or through a recording.

You might use this kind of meditation to help you:

- feel more relaxed
- find the answer to a question
- have a particular experience

Body scanning

One specific, easy type of mindful meditation is called a body scan.

This technique simply involves moving your awareness from one part of your body to the next, and tuning into the physical sensations of each body part. As you do this scan, notice where you're holding any tension and any feelings you become aware of as you connect with each body part.

You can do this in bed first thing when you wake up in the morning, or at night to help you drift off to sleep. You can even do it when you're waiting in line at the supermarket.

Wherever you do it, it's great to relax and move your awareness out of your head and into your physical body. It's a nourishing experience that brings you into a deeper relationship with both your authentic self and your body.

As with everything, there's no one right way to do it. I like to start at my toes and slowly work up my body. When I get to my shoulders, I go back down my arms to my fingers. Finally, I finish with my neck, head and face.

As you do this, you may notice areas that are stiff or tense. These feelings may be intense, or they can be subtle and hard to notice.

You may even become aware of emotions or memories as you connect to different parts of your body. This is because we can store our experiences in our bodies.

All of this is perfectly normal. Whatever you notice, try not to dwell on it. Simply acknowledge it and then keep moving through your body.

If you can't move on, and the feeling or memory is particularly persistent, it might have a message for you. In this case, ask it what it wants you to know. However, be aware that just like with your intuition, its message will only be positive or non-emotive.

Anything else is negative self-talk that you can move on from.

Nature walks

Being in nature has long been known to benefit our health and well-being. Cultures all over the world have sought out nature – from Victorians going to the seaside to convalesce through to the Japanese practice of *shinrin yoku*: forest bathing.

Being in nature can calm both your body and mind. The greens of the land and the blues of the water and sky are colours that have long been associated with the energy of healing.

Mind, a mental health charity in the UK, says on its website that the benefits of being in nature include helping you to:

- improve your mood

- reduce feelings of stress or anger

- feel more relaxed

- increase your confidence and self-esteem

- become more active

- connect to your local community

- reduce loneliness

Being in nature may even directly help some ailments, such as seasonal affective disorder (SAD) – a type of depression that usually affects people in winter.

When it comes to reclaiming your magick, spending time in nature can help you to feel more grounded and present. It can remind you of how connected we all are to the world around us.

We're often taught to think of nature as something that's 'out there'. But we ARE nature.

Yes, we can manipulate our environment. We can create houses, cities, technology and more.

I'm very glad that we can do all these things, but they can leave us feeling far removed from nature. And in disconnecting us from the nature outside, they can remove us from our own true natures.

Spending time in nature reminds us that we're part of it. We experience the same cycles of growth and decay. We're connected to, and governed by, the same seasons, And we're made up of exactly the same basic elements.

Tree hugging is a thing for a reason.

You may not be able to go for a walk in nature every day, but perhaps you have a garden you could step out into. Or maybe you have a balcony or a windowsill with plants on it. Even a single house plant that you can enjoy each day can be enough to remind you of, and connect you to, nature.

Activity: Nature bathing

Choose somewhere to go for a walk where you can surround yourself with nature. This could be a forest, a meadow, a lake shore, or even just standing by a tree.

Make sure you turn off any devices, so that you won't be disturbed.

Then slow right down. Breathe deeply and fully.

Start to move through nature deliberately.

Pay attention to anything you can feel and sense.

Take the time to stand still, sit or even lie down, and engage all of your senses.

Notice how you feel.

Observe the quality of your thoughts.

Try to witness things you've never noticed before. Become curious and explore your surroundings with fresh senses.

Look for the greens and blues that surround you, and let their presence soothe you.

Gaze into the distance, and let your eyes relax from all of the day-to-day tasks, which often require focusing on objects that are close up.

Stay in nature for as long as it feels comfortable.

Find the soul vitamins that work best for you... then use them

I know I keep saying this, but just as there's no one nutritional program that's right for everyone, there's no one right combination of soul vitamins either.

The only way to identify what works best for you is to try a range of different practices, let go of the things that don't work, and keep whatever does. Then, once you find something that works and feels right and aligned for you, commit to doing it.

Only with that repeated use will you experience the full benefits to build up the soul stamina you need to reach your desires and reclaim The Magick of You.

Key insights to take with you

- The habits that help you to achieve your desires come in two forms: some directly move you forward, and others make it easier to do those things.

- 'Soul vitamins' are the second kind – they're small, everyday habits and actions that you do regularly to support your physical, mental, emotional and magickal well-being.

- Much like with actual vitamins, you probably won't feel any change after 'taking one' the first time: experiencing the benefits requires repeated exposure.

- Some of my favourite soul vitamin habits include affirmations, mirror work, journaling, gratitude practices, visualisation, meditation and nature walks.

A question to think about

Which of the soul vitamin practices in this chapter immediately feel like they'd resonate most with you? Which are you willing to try, even if you're not sure they'd work for you?

4.4 How to Set Magickal Habits that Work for You

The paradox of structure

Considering how passionate I am about habits, it might surprise you to discover that I'm not a very habitual person. Well, not at first glance, anyway.

Every time I've tried to instil a habit the standard way, I've inevitably given up on it.

My why has been clear. My Magickal MIND mindset was in place. I knew what I needed to do, and I was completely committed to the outcome.

Despite all of this, conventional habit-setting just didn't work for me.

I might keep a routine in place for a week. In rare cases, I might manage it for a couple of months. Then, eventually, it would fall by the wayside.

It wasn't about my determination or my willpower. I *wanted* to keep doing the habit.

But something about scheduling an activity for the same time each week just drained my energy.

You might assume the issue was something to do with too much structure making me feel trapped. After all, I'm a creative and an intuitive.

That wasn't the problem, though. I love structure. It gives me a container to feel safe within. Knowing what's coming up can help me to relax into the process, instead of trying to control everything.

In fact, I think of structure – in the form of habits – as a riverbank that the river of my creativity and magick flows along. The riverbank gives the water form and a way to express itself. It holds the water, without necessarily restricting it.

For the river to flow freely and be supported, it needs the banks. In some places, it'll flow quickly in a rush of rapids. In others, it will peacefully roll along. Wherever it goes, it will always find its own rhythm and flow.

If the banks collapsed, the river would turn into a floodplain that could no longer express itself fully.

Your magick and creativity are the same. The structure within your magickal habits supports them, providing a sense of form to hold them. Like the river, sometimes you'll go fast, and sometimes you'll go slow, but you'll always find your own rhythm.

And again, just like the river, without any structure, your magick can't express itself.

I knew my problem with habits wasn't just about the structure they required. However, it wasn't until I started looking at different types of structure that I realised where the issue truly lay.

Find your own unique rhythm

My relationship with habits completely changed when I realised that rhythm was an essential element of structure... and a weekly rhythm just doesn't work for me.

Instead, I discovered that I had my *own* rhythm and flow. I began to trust that flow and work with it. Suddenly, the habits that I'd struggled to maintain for more than a couple of weeks became easier.

Like many people, I'd spent so much time working to everyone else's timelines and schedules that I'd forgotten I have my own rhythms. I have schedules and timelines that work best for me.

The benefits of magickal habits go beyond ensuring that *what* you'll do aligns with who you truly are. You can ensure that *when* you do it aligns as well. You have the opportunity to find your own rhythm and make the most out of it.

So many habit experts stress the importance of doing something daily to make it a habit. The truth is that you don't have to do anything daily. You just need to do it consistently, and you get to decide what consistently means to you.

Some habits might work perfectly for you to do daily at a specific time.

Others might work better weekly, monthly or even annually.

And still others might align better for you with the energy of some kind of natural cycle.

Do you flow better with cycles?

When I started getting to know my own rhythms and cycles better, I realised that a strict, calendar-based structure would never fit comfortably for me. Trying to do something at 2pm every Tuesday would never be sustainable.

I could force it for a while through sheer willpower, but it would drain my energy. I'd feel bad about not wanting to do the activity, then eventually give up.

Remember that magickal habits *shouldn't* feel like this. They aren't supposed to be a 'should'. If they start feeling this way, it's a sign that something about them needs refining.

And for me, that something was the timing.

I knew this, because as soon as I began to align my habits with the energy of my menstrual cycle, I had much greater success at being consistent. It allowed me to honour the natural ebb and flow of my personal energy, instead of trying to fight against it.

Once again, it's about flow, not force.

These days, to the external eye, my routine and habits may look completely unstructured. But from my perspective (which is the only one that matters for my own habits), they're in perfect harmony with my energetic, emotional, physical and spiritual health.

I can relax into the structure of my own rhythm.

Again, just because that's what works for me, it doesn't mean it will be right for you.

As always, experiment, try things out and see what supports you most.

Rhythms to explore for your habits

If you're like many people, you're used to living your life according to external, human-made rhythms. For example, in the Western world:

- days are divided into 24 hours
- weeks are divided into seven days
- months are divided into somewhere between 28-31 days
- years are divided into 12 months

Some of these divisions are loosely based on natural rhythms. For example, a calendar month is *around* the time it takes the moon to make a full orbit of the Earth. A year is *around* the time it takes the Earth to orbit the sun.

But of course, it's not an exact match, which is why we have different length months and leap years.

However, there are also many natural rhythms that exist in your life.

For example, days might not naturally divide up into hours, but they do divide into night and day. Years naturally divide up into moon cycles and seasons. If you have a menstrual cycle that's mostly regular, it can also create structure and rhythm in your life. Plus, most of us have a natural daily circadian rhythm that's calibrated to the amount of sunlight we get.

Here's how you can use a few of these natural rhythms to support your magickal habits.

Early birds and night owls

That circadian rhythm I mentioned above can work differently for different people.

'Early birds' or 'larks' naturally function best first thing in the morning. They'll easily wake up with the sun, and start to tire early in the evening.

Meanwhile, 'night owls' or just 'owls' have a body clock that's calibrated to start much later in the day. They prefer to sleep in, and then work later into the night.

For some reason, we have this idea in our culture that getting up early is a sign of virtue. Sleeping in because you worked late into the night, or just because you enjoy it, is seen as a moral failing.

I'm a night owl. Inspiration often strikes me in the early hours of the morning, and that's when my creative energy is usually at its peak. So I get a lot of work done then. Yet, at one point, I'd regularly find myself having to explain why I was still in bed late the next morning, lest people around me think I was lazy.

Unfortunately, many of the day-to-day structures in our culture just aren't set up to support night owls. If you have a regular 9-5 job or kids who need to be at day-care at a certain time, it can be impossible to live completely in tune with your natural cycle.

But to the best of your ability, give yourself permission to honour your own creative circadian cycle of ebb and flow.

The Moon and menstrual cycles

Before we had clocks and calendars, the moon was a natural reminder of the ebbs and flows of life over its 29.5-day cycle. And because menstrual cycles often have an approximately similar duration, the two have been linked throughout history.

That said, there's a lot of variation in individual menstrual cycles. So if your physical cycle phase doesn't line up with the moon's phase at some points, don't worry. Simply choose the cycle, whether it's lunar or menstrual, that your energy seems to align best with, and follow that one.

Both the moon and your menstrual cycle can be powerful allies to bring into your life to help you maintain your magickal habits.

The new moon and the menstrual phase

The new moon is usually associated with the first day of menstruation, which is the part of your cycle where you start actually bleeding.

This is the lowest energy point of both the lunar and menstrual cycles. It corresponds with resting and nourishing your body as you sink into the darkness and the mysteries of life.

It's the perfect time to build habits that relate to rest and connecting with your intuition.

The waxing moon and the follicular phase

The waxing moon is associated with the follicular phase of the menstrual cycle. If you menstruate, this is the phase where a new egg grows and ripens in your ovaries.

The energy at this stage of each cycle is growing and becoming bolder. It corresponds with exploring your pursuits at a deeper level and taking bold action.

The waxing moon or follicular phase is the perfect time to focus on creating systems and structures that support you, learning new things and connecting with new people.

The full moon and the ovulatory phase

The full moon is associated with ovulation, which is the menstrual phase where your body releases the ripened egg so it can travel to your uterus.

The energy during these phases is at its fullest peak. This corresponds with expressing yourself fully and enjoying your achievements.

The full moon or ovulatory phase is the perfect time to focus on habits related to completing tasks and projects, or being more social.

The waning moon and the luteal phase

The waning moon is associated with the luteal phase of a menstrual cycle. This is the phase where the egg waits for fertilisation. Eventually, your body expels it if that doesn't happen.

The energy at this stage of each cycle is beginning to turn inwards and wane. This corresponds with evaluating your life and releasing what no longer serves you.

The waning moon or luteal phase is the perfect time to build habits that involve letting go of old patterns that no longer serve or support you, or decluttering your space.

Days of the week

You may find that these natural cycles don't quite work for you either. Perhaps aligning habits with the new moon might make them too hard to plan for. In this case, maybe a bit of 'artificial', everyday structure could create some extra support for you.

Perhaps using energetic correspondences for the days of the week could help you bring some intention and magick to a habit. Traditionally, each day of the week has its own unique energy. Try tapping into these energies to support the magick that you weave in your life.

Monday

Monday is ruled by the Moon, which represents our emotions and intuition.

It corresponds with beauty, emotions, dreams, divination, fertility, illusion and insight.

It's the perfect day to connect with your intuition and get guidance on your focus for the week ahead.

Tuesday

Tuesday is ruled by Mars, the planet of energy and bold action.

It corresponds with courage, defence, protection, rebellion, strength, success and victory.

Make Tuesday your day to add some passion and drive to your week to get things done.

Wednesday

Wednesday is ruled by Mercury, the planet of communication and information.

It corresponds with the arts, change, creativity, communication and transportation.

Make Wednesday your day to express yourself fully and have those conversations you've been putting off.

Thursday

Thursday is ruled by Jupiter, the planet of abundance and expansion.

It corresponds with healing, prosperity, protection, strength and wealth.

Thursday is the day to learn new things and focus on what you want to expand in your life.

Friday

Friday is ruled by Venus, the planet of love and creativity.

It corresponds with birth, fertility, friendship, love, passion and romance.

This makes Friday the perfect time to relax and connect with others.

Saturday

Saturday is ruled by Saturn, the planet of structure and responsibility.

It corresponds with cleansing, protection, spirituality and wisdom.

This makes Saturday the perfect day to get productive and organised.

Sunday

Sunday is ruled by the Sun, which represents our expression and soul purpose.

It corresponds with prosperity, recognition, success and wealth.

Sunday is the perfect day to tap into your inner radiance and spirituality.

What's your perfect rhythm?

As you start setting magickal habits, you may want to experiment with different rhythms to find what works best for you. This is especially true if you have a previous pattern of not being able to make a consistent routine work for you.

You might even find that your natural rhythms align with longer cycles like the seasons. Maybe you find it easier to create cleaning habits in spring. How about maintaining more creative and expressive habits in summer? Or trying to create reflective habits such as meditation and journaling as the nights get longer in autumn and winter?

All of these options are OK and totally valid. Everyone's rhythms are different.

Try turning a habit into a ritual

For the longest time, people have found comfort in ritual, and have used it, knowingly or not, as a vehicle for magick. Ritual has allowed them to focus and direct their energy and intentions. It's helped to guide them into a deeper relationship with themselves and the world around them.

So it's not surprising that ritual can help you to maintain the magickal habits you want to build, and reconnect you more deeply with the Magick of You.

I'll talk a lot more about what, exactly, ritual is in *Section 5: Magickal Practices*. For the meantime, what I want you to know is that you can turn any habit or practice into a magickal ritual. Then, once you've done so, that activity can become an opportunity to:

- pause and listen closely for the messages your soul and intuition are whispering to you

- direct your energy in ways that align with those messages to bring you peace, power and purpose.

RIFF your rituals

You can turn anything into a ritual. You don't necessarily need to use special tools or dedicate lots of time to your ritual. Instead, you just need four things. And of course, I have an acronym handy to help you remember them:

Recognition

Pause, pay attention and recognise that you're about to turn an ordinary habit into something more meaningful to you.

Intention

Just like with your habits, you need to set a clear intention for the outcome you want to achieve through the ritual.

Focus

As you do your ritual, you need to focus all of your attention on what it is you're doing so that you can stay present as you do it. It's much like needing to be emotionally invested in your soul vitamins, rather than just checking them off like a to-do list.

Frequency

The more often you do your chosen ritual, the more meaning and connection you add to it, just as we explored in *Chapter 3.5 – The Dedicated MIND Mindset*.

Ritualising a habit can give it a greater sense of meaning and purpose, and then extend that meaning and purpose to your whole day if you want it to.

Bringing your focus and intention to an activity can turn even the most mundane of tasks into a ritual. Consider making one or more of these everyday tasks into rituals:

- going for a daily walk
- cooking a particular food
- creating art or music
- eating dinner with friends
- enjoying tech-free time
- having a bath or shower
- sipping your morning coffee

Activity: RIFFing an everyday ritual

This activity is very simple.

Identify an everyday habit you already have – perhaps getting dressed, eating breakfast, journaling or something from the list above.

Think about how you could RIFF it, then try it out and see how it feels.

We'll talk about how to combine a set of morning or evening habits into a beautiful, supportive ritual in the next chapter.

For the meantime, keep it simple and easy by just looking at a single habit.

Selecting your magickal habits

As I mentioned in the activity above, in the next chapter, I'll share more examples of magickal habits and practices you can combine to create morning and evening rituals.

Much like with the book as a whole, to get the most out of them, I recommend reading the chapter right through once from start to finish. This will give you a general feel for each practice and how you might adapt it to suit your needs and lifestyle.

Decide on the practices you want to try first, then re-read each practice in detail before you go ahead and try it. As always, simply knowing what to do isn't enough. You've got to actually do it.

They're called 'practices' because they're designed to be practised! And when you repeatedly practise them, they'll become your magickal habits.

Again, as we talked about in the Introduction, you can't just read a book to make progress with your fitness. You need to actually get out onto the gym floor. And, much like with a gym membership, it's not enough to go once (or even once a month) and then expect to see dramatic benefits. To get stronger or more flexible, you need to train regularly – at least two or three times a week, if not more.

It's exactly the same with creating your magickal habits. Plus, just like with gym training, the more often you practise your magickal habits, the more quickly they begin to feel natural and easy. They stop feeling like a big, dramatic hassle that demands a lot of preparation and figuring out.

They just become a natural part of your day that you slide into.

Key insights to take with you

- If you've struggled to make habits stick in the past, it might be because the structure you used wasn't right for you.

- Many of the rhythms we live our lives according to are artificial and don't work for everyone, but we also have natural rhythms in our lives.

- Try experimenting with different natural rhythms – for example, your circadian rhythm, lunar cycles or your menstrual cycle if you have one – as structures for your habits.

- Using focus and attention to turn mundane, everyday activities into rituals can also make them easier to maintain as magickal habits.

A question to think about

Which of the habits that you want to build feel like they'd most naturally align with becoming a ritual?

4.5 Magickal Mornings and Enchanted Evenings

In *Chapter 2.4 – Using Your Magickal Life Philosophy*, we looked at how something as simple as choosing your knickers can create more magick and meaning in your day. In this chapter, I want to explore more ways to add magick to otherwise ordinary habits.

Two great places to begin creating your magickal habits are at the beginning and the end of your day.

That's because thinking takes a lot of energy for your body and brain. So the more thinking you can take out of a routine you want to create, the easier that routine will be to do.

Unless you work nightshifts, you wake up each morning and go to bed each night.

(If you do work shifts, you can still use the techniques in this chapter. Just ignore what the rest of the world is doing, and define 'evening' as the time before you go to bed and 'morning' as the time after you wake up.)

Regardless of when you do them, waking up and going to bed are natural transitions in your day. So scheduling habits during these periods makes them easier for your body and mind to remember to do.

Magickal Mornings

Magickal Mornings give you the chance to start your day proactively instead of reactively. They give you a moment to think and explore how you feel and what you want to consciously create that day.

This allows you to start your day more mindfully and peacefully, compared to immediately getting caught up in the whirlwind of things that demand your time and attention.

As with everything in this book, there's no right way to create a Magickal Morning routine. Just a few options could include:

- no tech for the first hour of your morning

- any activities in your usual bathroom routine

- journaling or other soul vitamins
  (see *Chapter 4.3 – Soul Vitamin Habits*)

- taking a Sacred Pause
  (see *Chapter 4.6 – The Sacred Pause*)

Here's how a Magickal Morning might look if you bring your attention and focus to activities that are already part of your everyday morning routine. The advantage of this approach is that you can add a lot of focus and intention to your day without requiring much in the way of extra time.

Blessing your bathroom routine

You might start your Magickal Morning by taking a moment before you get out of bed to note down any dreams you remember.

You could then brush your teeth while focusing on the intention to remove the energy of any negative words you've thought about yourself or others. As you rinse off your toothbrush, you might then call in words of encouragement and support to replace those you removed.

If you have a mirror in your bathroom, you might add some mirror work after brushing your teeth, then end it – of course – with a cheeky wink.

If you intended to have a bath or shower that day, you could add some magick, awareness and intention to this without taking any extra time. As you stand under the water, you could imagine it washing away any of the energetic debris that dulls your shine or keeps you from expressing the Magick of You.

You could visualise anything that's not yours or any energy that isn't for your highest good being washed away down the plughole. Imagine your soap or shower gel cleansing away all the energetic dirt as well as the physical dirt.

Then, as you rinse away the soap, you could think about the qualities you'd like to experience more of in your day. These might be peace, joy, love, vibrancy – whatever they are, think about the colour you'd associate with each energy you want.

For example, you might associate green or blue with peace, and red or orange with vibrancy. So, as you stand in the shower, you could imagine the water becoming the colour you associate with what you want more of. Allow the colour to rain down over you, and let it fill you up with its energy.

As you focus on what you want to experience more of, know that you're attracting more of that energy in. It's like a full-body way to say, "Thank you, more please!" to your 'something bigger'.

I've listed a few other options below for activities to bring to your Magickal Morning routine. Try a few of them and see which ones resonate best for you.

Appreciating your body

Another option is to use your shower as an opportunity to connect with each area of your body.

To do this, consciously slow down the experience of washing yourself. Bring your full focus and attention to what you're doing. And as you wash each body part, thank it for all that it does for you.

As you wash your face, thank your senses for helping you to experience the world, and for the rich pleasure they bring you.

Thank your arms for all that they carry throughout the day, and for everything they help you to reach out towards.

Thank your hands for all they give and receive, and for all they create.

Thank your legs for their strength and their ability to move you through life. Thank your feet for helping you to 'take a stand' for what's important to you.

Thank your belly for all it absorbs and how it nourishes you.

Thank your skin for giving you a boundary and defining your space in the world.

Really take some time to show gratitude and appreciation for each part of your body.

Even if your body is a source of pain, thank it for doing the best it can.

Embodying words of affirmation

Once you're out of the bath or shower, you can use the act of applying skin care products as another way to connect with your body. As you apply your favourite oil, cream or lotion, take a moment to gently feel into and reconnect with your body.

Notice all of its curves, shapes and textures.

As you notice and touch each part of your body, say something kind and loving to yourself. Check out the section on affirmations in *Chapter 4.3 – Soul Vitamin Habits* for specific ideas on what to say.

Whatever words you choose, use them to create a more caring, nourishing relationship with yourself.

It doesn't matter whether you already love yourself deeply or feel completely disconnected from your body. You can always improve your relationship with it.

Choosing an intentional outfit

We talked about choosing your knickers intentionally back in *Chapter 2.4 – Using Your Magickal Life Philosophy*, but what about the rest of your clothes?

Do you have a top or a jacket that always makes you feel like you can take on the world? Maybe a piece of jewellery that makes you feel peaceful and connected to your inner wisdom? How about a particular shade of lipstick that makes you feel super confident?

Think back to the experiences you decided in the shower or bath that you wanted to attract more of into your life today. What clothes or accessories could you wear that would support that way of being and draw it to you?

Making a magickal cuppa

If you like to start the day with some kind of drink – tea, coffee or even just water – that's another opportunity to attract what you want to your day.

As you prepare your morning drink, think about what you'd like to experience more of over the coming day. Holding that thought in your mind, stir your drink in a clockwise direction nine times.

(In many paths, stirring clockwise represents attracting something into your life. If you stirred anti-clockwise with intention, it would represent removing something from your energy.)

Then, as you sip your drink, try using the moment as a mindful Sacred Pause, or perhaps do a form of journaling that suits you.

Enchanted Evenings

At the other end of the day, you can create an Enchanted Evening to help you wind down. It's often a good idea to create a balanced routine that includes nourishing your physical, emotional, mental and spiritual health.

Examples of activities you could bring in might include:

- physically, you could drink some water or do some gentle stretching
- emotionally, you could honour your feelings and let them flow
- mentally, you could journal about your day, listen to a podcast or read a book you enjoy
- spiritually, you could meditate or do your own form of spiritual practice

Winding down with intention

After you've finished all that you'll do that day, take time out to allow your body and mind to wind down. This sets a clear boundary between your time to be productive and your time to step into the energy of deep, nourishing rest.

Perhaps start by creating a space that's conducive to relaxing. This might include tidying up or doing some dishes. As you tidy, set the intention to create a distraction-free space where you can sink even deeper into the Magick of You.

Everything that's in your space attracts your attention, especially if you know you still have to do something with it. Once you've put an object away or completed a task, you 'close the loop' so it no longer distracts your energy.

Preparing for tomorrow

Next, you might want to start getting whatever you can ready for the next day. This means you can relax fully, knowing that everything is taken care of. Tasks for the evening might include:

- writing a to-do list (I've gone from hating these to loving them!)
- packing your bag so it's ready to grab and go the next day
- laying out your gym gear
- doing anything that will make your tomorrow slightly easier to slip into

Creating some ambience

Next, you might want to create a relaxing atmosphere in the space you'll spend your evening in.

You can bring all of your senses into this, but pay particular attention to the dominant sense we talked about back in *Chapter 1.2 – The Role of Intuition*. A few options might include:

- **Sight**: turn down the electric lights, and perhaps add a candle or two
- **Smell**: burn your favourite incense or diffuse essential oils
- **Taste**: sip a cup of your favourite herbal tea or some water
- **Sound**: play some relaxing music, or perhaps nature sounds
- **Touch**: change into some cosy, comfortable clothes that feel wonderful against your skin

Reconnecting with yourself and your body

In the last hour before bed, you could commit to either not scrolling social media or avoiding tech completely. This helps you to disconnect from other people's energy and attention so you can reconnect with your own energy and what's important to you.

This could also be the perfect time to do some journaling, allowing yourself to process the day and release anything that's bothering you. The SCAT process from *Chapter 4.3 – Soul Vitamin Habits* would be ideal for this. So would gratitude or appreciation journaling.

Next, you might want to do some light stretching to come back to your centre and reconnect with your body. And finally, you could choose to end your day reading a book you enjoy, or listening to your favourite meditation or podcast.

The more magickal habits you can put in place during the evening, the quicker you'll relax – and the better your rest and sleep will become.

Activity: Creating a magickal day

Your activity for this chapter is another simple one: to experiment with these ideas during your morning, evening or both.

Take what works for you. Leave the rest. The important thing is to create a routine that supports and serves you, and focuses you on what's important to you.

Try using your Magickal Life Philosophy and Magickal MIND mindset to select your perfect practices and timings.

Then focus on making each habit magickal to ensure it nourishes and supports the Magick of You.

Key insights to take with you

- The period just after you wake up and the period just before you go to bed are natural transition times.

- Scheduling habits during these times to create Magickal Mornings and Enchanted Evenings can make it easier to remember to do them.

- For Magickal Mornings, focus on habits that help you to bring more of what you want into the coming day.

- For Enchanted Evenings, focus on habits that help you to wind down, relax, recentre and reconnect with your body.

A question to think about

Which of the habits in this chapter calls out to you to try first?

4.6 The Sacred Pause

Why take a Sacred Pause?

Throughout much of your life, it can feel like you're being pushed and pulled in all sorts of directions. Sometimes, you might feel at the mercy of the demands or emotions of other people. Other times, it might be the events in your life that overwhelm you.

Either way, it's essential to have something you can do that brings you back to your centre and grounds you back into the present moment.

This allows you to connect to your magick and gives you a moment to catch your breath. From that space, you can respond constructively to the situation or person instead of reacting in a way that might not be as appropriate.

When I need something to ground me and create space around me in the moment, I take a Sacred Pause. I learnt this concept from Molly Remer, who in turn learnt it from Joanna Powell Colbert. As soon as I heard the term, my whole body sighed 'yesssss' in relief.

I loved finding a phrase that matched the energy I knew I needed – the energy that's essential for every one of us.

In a world that values doing and achieving, giving yourself a moment to step back and honour the need for space can be hard. Yet the Sacred Pause is the very essence of life.

Resting is as important as doing

I had this kind of Sacred Pause experience, although I didn't have a name for it then, when I started doing Kundalini Yoga.

I'd dabbled with yoga for years, but I'd always focused on doing it for fitness and flexibility. So when I started Kundalini Yoga, I was surprised to discover that we first held a pose and then rested for longer than we'd held it.

Initially, this frustrated me. I wanted to stretch and feel like I was 'doing' something.

But I chose to trust the process.

And I immediately noticed that in the rest within that pause, I could feel my energy releasing and moving around my body.

That's when I started to value the importance of the rest, rather than just the doing.

I realised that within the rest, I created space for the magick to happen.

Ever since then, I've honoured the concept that the pause is just as important as the doing. I've understood that we need both. That's why, when I heard Molly Remer use the term 'Sacred Pause', my body immediately recognised it as a moment to give myself space. It was a moment where nothing was expected of me, and my only task was to allow myself to be.

In that space, I could receive rest, nourishment and the guidance I sought.

I still tend to focus more on doing these days. But I also always ensure that I take moments to pause and check in with myself each day.

I pause to integrate my experiences and allow life and guidance to come to me.

How to take a Sacred Pause

One of the wonderful things about a Sacred Pause is that you can do it in a moment, even on the busiest of days. In fact, the practice can create a moment to cut *through* that noise and busyness and allow you to become present.

The challenge is to remember that this tool is available to you.

Whenever you feel overwhelmed, caught up in the energy of striving or anxious about the future, you can give yourself the gift of a Sacred Pause. This steps you out of your current experience of life. It gives you the space to consciously change how you feel.

It's also a useful practice even when you're *not* feeling overwhelmed. If you're caught up in routine, day-to-day activities such as working on your computer, cleaning or eating, the Sacred Pause creates a moment to check in with yourself.

It allows you to become present, notice how you're feeling and give your current task your full attention.

Stacking the pause

I'm a huge fan of 'stacking' your habits – adding new habits onto activities you already do.

Taking a Sacred Pause is a wonderful activity to stack on top of another daily habit you already have because you can do it anywhere, in any position. Regardless of whether you're standing up, sitting or lying down, you can take a moment to breathe and relax. That means:

- You can make your Sacred Pause the last thing you do before you get out of bed in the morning. Or you could make it the first thing you do after you lie down at night, or both.

- You can take a Sacred Pause after you get into your car and put on your seatbelt before you start each journey. And you can take another one when you arrive at your destination, after you turn off the engine but before you get out of the car.

- You can take a Sacred Pause before you start cooking your food, before you eat it and then again at the end of the meal.

- You can take a Sacred Pause at the beginning of a work task, and then again at the end. You can even take one at any time along the way when you feel tired, stuck or disconnected from the task.

There's no limit to the kinds of existing habits and activities you can stack a Sacred Pause on top of.

Activity: **Taking a Sacred Pause**

The easiest way to take a Sacred Pause is to close your eyes and put your hand over your heart space. This is the area of your energetic body that's just above the centre of your chest. It doesn't map exactly to the location of your physical heart, but it feels like your emotional centre.

Feel your body relax and let go of any thoughts or worries with every exhale.

Feel your shoulders drop, your jaw release, your teeth unclench and your eyebrows relax.

Feel your body and energy becoming softer.

With a bit of practice, you'll be able to do this in just a few breaths.

As you do, notice how your body feels.

Can you allow yourself to pause, or do you feel your activity or your day calling you to resume it?

Try to give yourself this moment to compassionately witness what's going on for you with no judgement.

Other ways to take a Sacred Pause

There are many ways to take a Sacred Pause. I've listed a few other suggestions below, but – as always – get creative and do whatever works for you. Remember that a practice only works when you do it, so pick something you find simple and fun.

It's worth practising each of the techniques you like to see which ones are the most effective for you in various situations. You'll likely find that you prefer one technique in one situation, and another in a different setting.

You'll also probably discover a favourite technique that becomes your go-to Sacred Pause.

Here are a few options to try.

Explore what you need

Sometimes, the simple act of asking yourself what it is that you need right now can bring you back into the moment.

Try placing your hand over your heart space to connect with your body, and asking yourself:

- What do I need right now?

- What can I give myself right now to feel fully satisfied?

- What do I need to make myself feel complete right now?

Notice that these questions focus on what you can do for yourself, not what you want others to do. They also avoid aiming for intensely positive emotions like happiness or joy, which can be an unrealistic stretch, and even harmful, if they're not your authentic truth.

Like everything else in this book, this isn't about toxic positivity or emotional bypassing. It's about experiencing authentic presence, acceptance and completion in the context of whatever's real for you right now.

Say your affirmations

As we explored in *Chapter 4.3 – Soul Vitamin Habits*, taking a moment to say your affirmations helps you to re-align your energy.

Additional affirmations that you could try during a Sacred Pause include:

- I'm learning to trust myself completely.
- I'm starting to find creative solutions to challenges I encounter.
- I'm becoming more connected to my inner-most truth.
- Each day I feel more supported in every decision I make.
- With every inhale, I receive love and nourishment.
- I'm starting to choose positive habits that support me.
- I'm learning to prioritise myself and my needs with love and ease.

Strike a power pose

Power poses are stances or gestures that let you take up space. You can see this 'in the wild' when runners throw their arms up in the air as they cross the finish line. You can also see it when someone pumps their fist skyward to celebrate achieving something important to them.

According to research from Amy Cuddy, power poses also reduce the stress hormone cortisol and increase your confidence on a physical level. (Amy has a fabulous TED talk on power poses that I recommend checking out to fully understand their value.)

Mentally, striking a power pose reminds you to take up space with your thoughts, feelings, dreams, decisions and physicality. And from an energetic point of view, power poses expand your energy field, which again, creates space for you to think, feel and dream.

In *Chapter 2.2 – Getting Full of Yourself*, we started to talk about how ingrained being small is in our culture. We discussed how that message keeps us from taking up space and expressing ourselves fully. For too long, people – in particular, women – have been told that they're too much. They're too loud, too emotional, too high-maintenance, too... something.

Society constantly tells us that our value lies in being small, both physically and behaviourally. In fact, we're regularly judged by our body size: the smaller we are, the more acceptable and worthy we are. Why else would the weight loss and diet industry be worth $192.2 billion in 2019 and still be growing quickly, according to Allied Market Research?

But being small goes beyond body size. Women are told to 'act ladylike', which usually involves being meek, demure and undemanding. It means putting other people first, and staying quiet about anything that may inconvenience others or make them feel uncomfortable.

It means not causing a fuss.

So, right now, I want you to take up space. Take up ALL of the space around you. Make yourself as big as you physically can, and notice how it makes you feel.

Give yourself permission to keep on physically taking up space.

I know many people who go off to the bathroom to strike a power pose before an important interview or work meeting.

Even if you don't have much time, you can:

- start your day with a power pose
- strike one whilst you're still in bed
- try one when you're in the shower

How to strike a power pose

Try raising your hands above your head and out to the side, or place your hands on your hips.

(When I hold my hands above my head, it feels like I'm funnelling all the energy of my magick down to me. When I put my hands on my hips, I feel as if I'm making a statement to the world – something like 'You'd better believe this is happening!')

Stand with your feet further apart than your hips and allow yourself to take up space.

Some people I know do this pose in bed and call it their Starfish pose.

If you have any mobility issues, just imagine yourself holding the power pose. You'll still experience the benefits.

Try out different poses to see how each feels for you. If they feel different, you may decide to use each one for a different purpose.

Hold your pose for as long as it feels right to you.

I set a phone timer for two minutes, which seems like a great amount of time to experience the pose's benefits for me.

Try experimenting and hold the pose for more or less time to see what works for you.

Read your favourite quote or poem

A book of your favourite quotes and poems is a great tool for creating a Sacred Pause.

Simply grab your book, flick it open to a random page and allow yourself to be moved and inspired by your favourite writers.

You could even write your own words of wisdom to inspire yourself during your Sacred Pause moments.

Create a Book of Brilliance

Magickal people often keep a Book of Shadows to record all of their magickal workings. Alongside this, I recommend also creating a 'Book of Brilliance' that focuses on all the brilliance and joy you create and encounter as you move through your life.

To make your book, take a journal and – if you wish – decorate it in a way that feels great to you. Then add in pictures, quotes, poems, affirmations and experiences that add to the energy of living a brilliant and magickal life.

When you want to take a Sacred Pause, try reading back through your Book of Brilliance. Let it remind you of the things you love that inspire you, and let the reminder bring you back to your centre.

Drink a cup of tea or coffee

In the previous chapter, we talked about turning the act of drinking your daily cuppa into a magickal habit. I mentioned that you could also make it into a moment of Sacred Pause.

To do this, once you've made your morning brew, sit down and drink it with intention.

Breathe its aroma in deeply, then exhale again slowly.

Savour its taste, being present as you take each sip.

Notice its flavour, its fragrance, its temperature and even its texture.

Slow down and be present with yourself and the moment.

Try the Emotional Stress Release technique

One technique I learnt during my kinesiology training was Emotional Stress Release (ESR). In fact, on the very first day of our training, before the course had even begun, our tutor had us all do this exercise without telling us what we were doing.

She explained that she always did this with new students to reduce their stress in starting something new... and it worked!

The exercise comes in two parts. The first part is great if you're short of time, or feeling light-headed or dizzy. The second part reduces stress and overwhelm.

You *can* do the first part on its own, but it's more powerful if you combine the two parts.

Part one

Before you start the practice, give yourself a score out of 10 for how you feel right now. Use a scale where 0 means cool as a cucumber, and 10 means the red mist has descended, and you can't think straight.

Then tap on your chest in an anti-clockwise direction for about 30 seconds.

This will help to rebalance your energies.

Next, hold the reflex points on your head (see Figure 1: reflex points) and think about something that's bothering you in as much detail as possible.

Think about who was there, what was said, what else happened and exactly how you felt. The more you feel as you remember this situation, the more energy you can release.

Then, simply hold the reflex points for a couple of minutes.

When you're ready to stop, check how you're feeling again on the scale of 0 to 10.

You can hold the points for as long as you need to, but don't feel as though you have to keep going until you've hit 0. Sometimes, just moving a few points, perhaps from an 8 to a 5, is enough to be able to continue without feeling consumed by emotion.

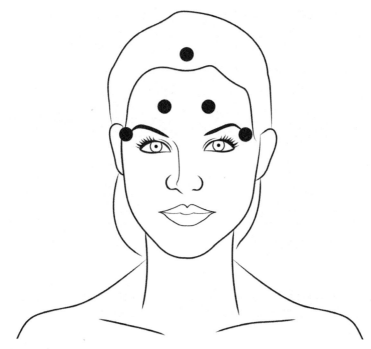

Figure 1: reflex points

Part two

Hold the five reflex points in Figure 1:

- one point at either temple
- one point at each frontal eminence
- one point at the anterior fontanelle

The easiest way to hold these points on yourself is to place:

- your thumbs on your temples
- your little fingers on your frontal eminences
- your index or middle finger on your anterior fontanelle.

Hold these points for a few minutes, or until you start to feel calmer.

Building a Sacred Pause into your spiritual routine

You can also stack the Sacred Pause practice on top of your existing spiritual routines and practices.

Add it to your daily devotional

If you have a daily spiritual practice, it most likely already contains a moment of Sacred Pause within it. If not, you can easily add one.

For example, you can include a moment of inner reflection, meditation or prayer.

Or you can light a candle with the intention of bringing yourself clarity and calm.

Take a moment to explore which techniques would resonate best with your individual practice.

Use tools alongside a Sacred Pause

You can use your favourite magickal tools when you take your Sacred Pause.

For example, you might draw a daily oracle card, charm or rune to seek guidance for your day. If so, before you draw, you could take a moment to breathe and feel your energy centre itself as you become more present.

Then ask your question or just ask for general guidance, and draw your selected item.

Spend a few mindful moments reflecting on the message you've received.

You may want to note down your messages to look for themes as the days and weeks go by.

Practise a range of techniques before you need them

It's a good idea to practise using the techniques you're drawn to during times when you don't actually *need* a Sacred Pause.

This gives you a chance to figure out which technique will work best for you when you're not already feeling stressed or overwhelmed.

That way when you do need the pause, you'll already know how to best create the space you need. This means you won't have to spend time and energy figuring out which technique to use when you're in the middle of the situation.

Instead, you'll just be able to slip into a moment of Sacred Pause and let the space it brings expand around you.

Key insights to take with you

- While taking a Sacred Pause may seem like a tiny thing, it can be an essential practice to avoid getting caught up in, or overwhelmed by, life.

- When it comes to using your magick to bring your dreams and desires into reality, resting is as important as doing.

- Taking a Sacred Pause can be as simple as reconnecting with yourself for a few deep, mindful, intentional breaths.

- You can also stack a Sacred Pause onto other everyday habits, bring it into your spiritual routines or add tools to the practice.

A question to think about

Which Sacred Pause techniques work best for you in which situations?

Section 5: **Magickal Practices**

Rituals that help you to connect with the Magick of You

5.1 Bringing it All Together with Magickal Practices

Practices and rituals connect you with the Magick of You

You've identified the Magickal Life Philosophy you want to use to guide your life, and the Magickal MIND mindset and practical magickal habits you need to support that philosophy.

Now, it's time to bring it all together.

In this section, we're going to talk about magickal practices and rituals. I'll also introduce you to two favourites, both for me and for my clients. These practices help to not only stop that steady drip, drip, drip of power erosion we talked about back in the Introduction, but also to actively fill you back up again.

So, much like we discussed back in *Chapter 2.2 – Getting Full of Yourself*, they help you to reconnect with who you truly are and what you truly want. Not just once, in a moment of insight and epiphany, but regularly, over and over again, until it's hard to believe you were ever disconnected.

Better yet, they go beyond helping you to *know* who you are and what you want. They actively help you to align with the energy of both, moving you towards creating the results you want. And what is that, if not connecting with the Magick of You?

Before we dive into the specific practices though, I want to spend a moment looking at the difference between habits, which we covered in *Section 4: Magickal Habits*, and practices or rituals.

These are just my definitions: if you want to define any or all of these terms differently, go right ahead. Fair warning: the boundaries between the three can be fuzzy... but when I think about each one, here's where I see the lines sitting:

- A **habit** is a single action you repeat so often that it becomes – if not automatic, then at least easy. Once you get your habit going, you don't have to think about it: you just do it. We talked about habits like taking a shower, making a morning drink or journaling in the evening in the previous section.

- A **practice** can be either a single action or a combination of connected actions that you regularly repeat with a specific intention to give it meaning. For example, you might have a general habit of taking a daily shower. Then, once a week, you might create a practice of bringing conscious intention and meaning to that shower. Perhaps you use it to wash away all the energy you've collected that's not yours, and then start afresh.

- A **ritual** is very much like a practice, but with a more spiritual twist – whatever 'more spiritual' might mean for you. I'm a firm believer that almost everything can be spiritual, so I use the terms 'practice' and 'ritual' interchangeably. But if your approach to life involves a separation between the spiritual and physical worlds, or you're just uncomfortable with the word 'ritual' generally, feel free to substitute whatever works best for you.

Ritual and community

Another piece of the puzzle that I use to help me differentiate a ritual from a practice in my own mind is the idea of community.

A practice is something I do individually on my own, independent of anyone else. If a practice is a shared one – something I take comfort in doing because it connects me to others who are doing exactly the same thing, maybe even at the same time – I'm more likely to think of it as a ritual.

For example, if I *were* a Christian, reciting the Lord's Prayer in church as we talked about in *Chapter 3.4 – The Nourished MIND Mindset* might be a ritual for me. Or, if I were Jewish, lighting the Sabbath candles on a Friday night might be a ritual. The act would connect me to not only other people lighting Sabbath candles now, but to my ancestors who've done the same thing in generations before me.

And as a Modern-Day Witch, setting an intention on the new moon is definitely a ritual for me.

In my own life, I think of the practices I'm going to share with you in the next two chapters as rituals because I do them each week alongside others in my community. Doing the practice together creates a deeper, more meaningful experience of the ritual for all of us. Perhaps it's about knowing that we're each adding to the collective energy of the ritual.

In the end, the wording is up to you

It's probably not a good idea to get too caught up in the terminology. What you call something matters far less than whether you do it regularly, and whether you pay attention to its effects in your life when you do.

Yes, for the most part, habits are simpler and more automatic. So if something involves multiple steps or actions, or requires conscious intention, it's probably a practice or a ritual.

But practices and rituals *can* also be simple, single actions if you want them to be. So the way I see it, brewing yourself a morning coffee could equally be a habit, a practice or a ritual, depending on how you approached it.

Just use the wording that works best for you and move on to the doing part.

Introducing my two favourite magickal rituals: GRACE and SACRED

I mentioned above that I'm going to talk about two of my favourite rituals in the chapters that follow this one. These are the regular go-to practices I use to connect to my own magick by:

1. letting go of everything that doesn't serve or support me

2. filling myself up with what does, and then

3. embodying and amplifying my magick to create what I want in my life.

I call these rituals the GRACE and SACRED practices.

And yes, of course they're acronyms (this is me, after all). Although hopefully, they'll help you to show yourself some grace and remember your own sacredness too.

Note: if you've read my previous book, Ditch the Doubt, *you'll recognise both rituals from there. In that book, however, I introduced them in the context of helping you to make better, clearer, more confident decisions. So, in* Ditch the Doubt, *I suggested SACRED as an ideal element of your Magickal Morning routine, and GRACE as a perfect part of your Enchanted Evening.*

But the joy of a great ritual is that it can help you to accomplish more than one thing, and create more than one benefit. So all I needed to do was tweak each ritual very slightly, and they became just as helpful in reconnecting me with my magick.

These days, I use the GRACE practice to help me let go of what I need to and then fill myself up again. After that, the SACRED practice helps me with the embodying and amplifying part.

As with any practice I recommend to you though, it's important to realise they're not strict process diagrams. I'm not giving you a recipe where you have to follow every specific step to the letter, using the exact same ingredients I use, to get a perfect result.

Instead, what I'm doing is suggesting a set of general steps that you can follow in whatever way, and to whatever degree, they work for you. If something in the process doesn't work for you, either try substituting something else, or leave that thing out altogether.

Don't be afraid to experiment, play and explore. The only 'wrong' way to do either ritual is the one that doesn't work for you. So do all of it, do none of it, or do anything in between.

Whatever you choose, it's your journey.

Getting the most from GRACE and SACRED

While I've just said that there's no wrong way to do these rituals, as with the rest of the book, I do think it's useful to read through each one from start to finish first. That will give you a feel for what's in each practice, and get you thinking about how you might adapt it to suit your individual needs and lifestyle.

Then give yourself a moment to feel into which of the rituals you want to try first. Yes, you can absolutely do them both if you want to. But you might find it easier to pick one and get to grips with it by doing it a few times before you move on to the next.

When you actually try out the ritual, you'll probably find things that made perfect sense or seemed like they'd flow smoothly when you first imagined them, which just don't work for you in practice. You might also find yourself getting an intuitive 'nudge' to substitute something you'd decided to do for something else, or to leave something out.

All of that is totally normal and totally fine. As I said above, experiment, play and explore. Who knows what you'll end up discovering and creating?

Take time out after each ritual to record it

Another thing I recommend to people who do the SACRED or GRACE rituals with me is to take a few minutes afterwards with their journals to record:

- how they felt before the ritual
- what they did during it, including anything they decided to change up last-minute
- anything they noticed during it, including how they felt
- anything they noticed after it – again, including how they felt

That's because, in our busy lives, it's all too easy to move straight from the sacred 'time out' of a ritual into the hustle and bustle of everyday work, without taking a pause.

Quite aside from the sense of emotional whiplash this can cause, it can also make it hard to remember what worked for you in the ritual and what didn't. Reconnecting with your magick involves constantly learning, growing and evolving. As you do, a technique that's worked just fine for you for weeks or months can suddenly become less effective. Briefly jotting down whatever you noticed during and after the ritual helps you to:

- quickly spot if something's no longer working for you, so you don't keep on doing it
- start thinking about how you might want to change it up next time you do that ritual.

Plus, journaling can make you more likely to notice the subtle progress you make as you become more full of yourself and start moving towards your dreams and desires.

If you don't already have a notebook you want to use for this, I recommend just finding something you enjoy writing in. As with the other journals we've talked about earlier in the book, it doesn't have to be anything fancy or expensive. It just needs to have paper that feels good to write on.

Although, of course, if you *want* to treat yourself to something special, that's fine too!

And, as we talked about in the Journaling section of *Chapter 4.3 – Soul Vitamin Habits*, you don't *have* to use pen-and-paper. You can record your thoughts and everything you notice digitally if that works better for you.

Activity: Recording your weekly (or monthly) progress

In addition to recording what you notice immediately after the ritual, I recommend making a regular time each week, or perhaps each month, to reflect on your progress. During this, ask yourself questions like:

- How did the quality of your energy change from day to day and week to week? What might have influenced that?

- Did you feel more aligned, fulfilled and on-purpose on some days compared to others? What might have influenced that?

- Did you find yourself feeling more connected to the Magick of You on some days compared to others? What might have influenced that?

- Which days could you be more present for yourself, your friends and your family? What might have influenced that?

- Which days did you feel more satisfied with your progress? Which days left you feeling frustrated or 'less than'?

- How did you honour your needs and desires? When did you speak up for yourself and your boundaries?

- How, and how much, did other people's moods, comments or actions affect you?

- How often, and how easily, did you find yourself saying no when you needed to?

- How did you navigate any potential obstacles? What were the results?

You don't have to make this a long, in-depth process – although again, if you want to spend longer than usual on it, feel free to.

You don't have to answer every single one of these questions every time you sit down to reflect, either. Perhaps glance over the list, and answer the three or four questions that seem most relevant on that day.

The key is to approach this reflection with a sense of curiosity, rather than judgement about what you think you should have done. Don't make yourself wrong for having bad days. We all do, and sometimes we can learn more from them than we do from when everything goes perfectly.

Whatever you feel is fine. Just be honest with yourself, and be willing to appreciate and celebrate every little insight.

Remember that, above all, it's a practice

Once again, we call GRACE and SACRED 'practices' because they're only helpful when we practise them regularly. Much like with soul vitamin habits, doing them once won't (usually) work miracles.

Instead, results come from repeated, sustained practice. One benefit of doing weekly or monthly reflections is that you'll start to see your progress slowly building over time.

Plus, many of my clients tell me that while it feels good as they do each ritual, they don't realise the true benefits until they stop.

Suddenly, they start to doubt and second-guess themselves in areas they'd been confident in the week before. And they wouldn't have noticed the link without some kind of regular reflection practice that kept them checking in with themselves.

Key insights to take with you

- Magickal practices or rituals are either single actions or combinations of connected actions that you repeat regularly with intention to give them meaning.

- They can help you to connect to the Magick of You by reconnecting you with who you are and what you want.

- Even more powerfully, they can help to align you with the energy of both, which can support you in creating the results you want.

- Two of my favourite magickal rituals are called GRACE and SACRED, and I'll introduce you to each of them in the next couple of chapters.

- You can choose to try one, both or neither – and if you try either of them, I recommend taking time afterwards to note down your experiences.

A question to think about

What magickal rituals or practices do you already do in your daily life? What benefits do you get from them?

5.2 | The GRACE Practice

Overview – why give yourself GRACE?

Back in *Chapter 1.3 – Understanding Energy*, we talked about the energetic smog that everyone else's thoughts, beliefs, judgements and priorities create around you. And I mentioned that the answer to clearing away that smog – for both me and many of my clients – is the GRACE practice.

So in this chapter, I'm going to take you through the five steps of the practice. I'll explain how each one helps in the journey of:

- releasing everything that's getting in the way of connecting with the Magick of You to create energetic closure
- appreciating and celebrating yourself for everything you are and everything you've done
- becoming full of your own essence and priorities again to ground yourself in your power

To help you do this, the GRACE practice consists of five steps:

- **GROUND** your energy and become present to bring closure to everything that's outstanding.
- **RECOGNISE** all that you've achieved since the last time you did the ritual, savouring your accomplishments so you can build on them.
- **APPRECIATE** yourself for who you are and take time to really honour how you've shown up in the world since you last did the practice.

- **CALL BACK YOUR ENERGY** from external people, events or situations, so you can move forward free from their influence.
- **EMBODY** your truth to become so full of your own dreams and desires that you leave no room for other people's expectations and judgements.

We'll talk through each of these steps in more depth over the rest of this chapter, but know that you can make them as simple or complex as you'd like.

The best time to practise GRACE

As with everything else in the book, there's no one right way to do this practice. You can try adding, changing or leaving out any part of it to see how that works for you.

The same is true of *when* you do it. I love practising GRACE as a ritual with my community at the end of each week to reset my energy and get me ready for a fresh start in the coming week. You might find it works better for you at the beginning of the week, or on a more or less frequent basis. For example, you might try using it:

- **daily each morning**, if your life is particularly full of energetic smog, and you need a touchpoint each day to shed it and reconnect with yourself
- **daily each evening**, if you regularly build up a tangle of unhelpful energetic cords over the day and think ritually releasing them might help you sleep more peacefully
- **monthly**, perhaps each new moon, if you have less energetic clutter to cut through, or find yourself naturally clearing it and filling yourself up without conscious practices

The key is to figure out a schedule that works for you at this point in your life and then try it for a while, noting down whatever you discover.

If the first schedule you try works for you, keep using it. If not, figure out why not and adjust.

What to expect once you've finished

Working through the GRACE ritual helps to naturally, gently dissolve old energetic patterns that have been blocking you from connecting with and living the Magick of You. Practising it regularly gives you the tools to re-align yourself with your own truth, energy and values.

So by the time you get to the end, you can expect to feel at least a little:

- more full of yourself, with all the confidence, clarity and certainty that fullness brings

- less swayed or upset by other people's thoughts, judgements and beliefs about what you 'should' want from your life, and how you 'should' go about getting it

- more at peace with, and accepting of, the perfectly imperfect elements of yourself that might have felt like flaws to fight against in the past

- less bothered by, and judgemental of, the flaws and imperfections of other people around you

- clearer and more refreshed and renewed, as though you just took an energetic shower

It's OK if you don't feel like this every time, though. Much like with the soul vitamins in *Chapter 4.3 – Soul Vitamin Habits*, sometimes the effect can be subtle. It's often only through repeated practice that you'll notice how the ritual is helping you to connect with and embody your magick.

Whatever you notice, just keep tracking and recording it, then adjusting if necessary.

And if you'd like to follow along with the GRACE practice in real-time, visit www.RebeccaAnuwen.com/MagickalBonuses to access videos of the practice.

Step 1: Ground

The first step of the GRACE practice is to ground your energy and become present.

Grounding is essential because so many of us spend most of our time focusing on either the past or the future. We think about things we've done, and how we wish we – or someone else – had done them differently. Or we plan out everything we want to get done, or worry about how we'll cope if things don't go the way we want them to.

There's nothing wrong with reflecting on previous events to learn from them, or setting intentions for what you want to happen. But devoting all your energy to the past or future leaves you very little time to experience the present moment. It can also distract you from connecting with how you feel right now and what you actually want or need in this moment.

You might also find yourself feeling scattered, distracted, powerless, unsafe and stuck in your head. Excess energies from anxiety or overwhelm can crackle and buzz through your system like lightning, leaving you feeling 'fried'.

Grounding yourself in the present moment is like a 'lightning rod' for those excess energies. It can help you to neutrally witness and observe events instead of getting caught up in storms of judgement or blame. And it creates a foundation for all the other steps in the rest of the practice.

Activity: Grounding yourself in the present

The quickest way to ground yourself is to simply close your eyes, put your hand over your heart space and take a couple of slow, deep breaths.

Much like with a Sacred Pause, that's all there is to it. Here's why this helps:

- Closing your eyes helps you shut out the world around you. When you close off your visual sense, it's easier to notice what you're feeling in the moment.

- Placing your hand over your heart space moves you out of your mind and connects you with what's going on in your body.

- Breathing slowly and deliberately helps to calm your nervous system, creating a sense of peace and well-being. (There's a reason that so many meditation practices across different cultures begin with the breath.)

Keep focusing on each inhale and exhale until you feel your energy begin to calm and return to your body. If you notice your thoughts shifting to something in the past or future, just gently bring them back to your breath again.

If you feel uncomfortable, remind yourself that you're safe and that whatever you experience is OK.

Other grounding techniques

If you struggle to simply focus on your breath, try adding one or more of these activities.

If you're grounding indoors

- Sit with your feet flat on the floor and connect with the energy of the Earth below you.
- Massage or rub your physical body to help you become aware of it.
- Dance or stomp your feet.
- Drum (the deeper the sound of the drum, the better).
- Make deep, guttural noises with your voice.
- Place a rock, stone or pebble by your feet.
- Wear red socks – yes, really!

If you're grounding outside

- Walk around barefoot in the grass, sand or mud.
- Lie with your back flat on the Earth.
- Paddle in the ocean.
- Notice and become present to the weather elements around you.
- Stand with your back against a tree (or turn around and hug it).

Step 2: Recognise

The next step of the GRACE practice is to recognise yourself.

The world we live in values doing and achieving above everything else. Success is too often measured by what you've done and achieved, not by what you've contributed or enjoyed.

So, at the end of the day or week, if you still have tasks left on your to-do list, they become the focus. All the things you *have* ticked off just fall by the wayside.

Perhaps you've accomplished something really significant. You might have completed a course, got a new job or achieved a long-held goal. Instead of taking the time to truly savour your triumph, though, you just move straight on to the next thing on your list.

Of course, accomplishments don't always have to involve doing something major. Sometimes, the biggest achievements are about consciously choosing NOT to do something. Perhaps you said no to an opportunity or prioritised your rest.

Society doesn't generally see these types of accomplishments as worth recognising. But, as we've already talked about, they're essential to acknowledge.

Noticing everything you've done also gives you a sense of identity as a unique individual. It's easy to lose this sense of yourself, especially if you've recently been through a major life event such as getting married or divorced, having a baby, changing your job or retiring.

And finally, recognising yourself helps you to remember everything you do as a person – everything you contribute to your own life and the lives of those around you. It's hard to celebrate the unique Magick of You if you don't recognise where it's already at play in your life. Acknowledging everything you've done helps you to notice this.

Recognise ALL your different accomplishments

Accomplishments come in different shapes and sizes, and it's important not to discount any of them. Once you start to mindfully recognise all you've done during your day, you'll be surprised by how much of it there is.

I like to split recognising into four areas, which will be familiar from the Celebrate section of the SCAT journaling activity in *Chapter 4.3 – Soul Vitamin Habits*. As a reminder, these are:

- **The major things you've accomplished**: the things most people typically think of when they hear the word 'accomplishment'. They might be major to-do list items, significant wins or activities that required you to step out of your comfort zone.

- **The everyday tasks you've crossed off**: the many small, routine 'adulting' tasks that require little thought, but still take energy and time to complete. They might include anything you do to maintain your home or make your life run more smoothly.

- **The ways in which you supported other people**: any times that you've given your energy, resources or time to help other people – perhaps a friend, your partner or a cause you care about.

- **The ways in which other people supported you**: this may seem counter-intuitive to list as an accomplishment, since it's about what someone else has done for you. But people can't show up for you unless you first create and nurture a relationship with them, and you have to actively accept their support.

For more specific examples of accomplishments or achievements to recognise and celebrate, check out the SCAT journaling activity.

Activity: Recognising yourself

Place your hand over your heart and run through each of the sections above, one by one.

As you do, really allow yourself to savour all that you recognise about yourself.

Let your recognition encompass everything you've done, from the small, everyday adulting tasks, to the actions that have stretched you and made you grow.

As you do, also recognise all the ways in which you've taken a stand for yourself and made time for what's important to you (which might have meant choosing *not* to do something).

Above all, remember that recognition isn't just about achieving and doing. It's also about being and brewing. As we discussed in *Chapter 4.6 – The Sacred Pause*, creating space and taking a rest is every bit as important as taking action.

If you're not currently doing SCAT journaling as a soul vitamin habit, you may also want to dedicate a special journal to documenting all that you recognise about yourself.

Then, whenever you feel that you're not where you 'should' be, you can take a moment to read back through everything you've accomplished. This can also be helpful to remind yourself of what you've already done any time you feel like you'll never complete your to-do list.

Either way, you'll soon be re-inspiring yourself.

Step 3: Appreciate

The next step in the GRACE practice is to appreciate yourself.

After spending some time recognising all that you've done for yourself and others, you'll hopefully be starting to feel good about yourself.

Now, I want you to take this to the next level, and begin to appreciate yourself for *who you are*.

This is about building on the energy of recognition to appreciate and admire your inherent qualities, above and beyond what you've done.

We talked about practising gratitude and appreciation generally back in *Chapter 4.3 – Soul Vitamin Habits* too. But just for this practice, I want you to focus on appreciating YOU.

It's far too easy to judge yourself, compare yourself to others and measure your achievements by someone else's ideas of success. That's even truer in the world of social media, where it's easy to confuse the unedited mess of your real life with the filtered highlight reel of someone else's.

This kind of judgement makes it easy to slip into patterns of self-criticism. To step you out of the energy of comparison and wanting, it's important to appreciate yourself just as you are.

It's time to break those disempowering patterns and replace them with kindness, self-compassion and dare I say it... self-love.

We're all messy, complicated, paradoxical humans with our own sets of quirks. In fact, those quirks are what make us wonderful, unique and worthy of appreciation.

So take the time to really appreciate yourself and all you are, including:

- **your unique values and way of seeing the world**: without them, you simply wouldn't be who you are.

- **your approach to life**: you may not see it as perfect, but whose version of perfect are you comparing it to?

- **your body**: again, you may feel it's not perfect, but whose version of perfect is your baseline? If parts of your body don't work well or are in pain, try to recognise the parts that are healthy. Don't try to pretend that your body's perfect as it is, but show it some much-needed love and compassion anyway.

Try to even appreciate how fabulous you are at your less-than-helpful habits (like noticing every single mistake you make), while at the same time, working to upgrade those habits.

Appreciating yourself helps you to fill yourself up with your own love and approval, leaving less room for the need for external validation to creep in.

Activity: Appreciating yourself

Take another deep breath and ask yourself what you can appreciate about yourself today. Perhaps it might be:

- the joy and humour you bring to your own day, and to other people around you

- your skill at baking your favourite cake

- your courage in taking a stand for yourself or something that's important to you

- your willingness to choose to do something that you don't enjoy now but that your future self will thank you for

- the benefit you enjoyed today because your past self was willing to choose what was right for you, instead of taking the easy option

- the pleasure you experience from simply wearing your favourite clothes

Whatever you identify to appreciate about yourself, allow yourself to savour that appreciation. Spend some time feeling awe about who you are and everything that makes you YOU.

Once again, you may want to write down all that you appreciate about yourself in your journal to brighten your day whenever you feel 'less than'.

Other ways to appreciate yourself

Sometimes, taking tangible action can help to boost your appreciation for yourself. Try:

- letting yourself receive other people's appreciation by writing down all the appreciative acts or words they offer you

- writing down at least three things that you appreciate about yourself each day

- repeating affirmations that carry the energy of appreciation (see the section on affirmations in *Chapter 4.3 – Soul Vitamin Habits* for ideas)

- thanking yourself for any reason, or no reason at all

- doing something kind for yourself

- taking yourself out on a date or buying yourself a gift

- giving yourself something you want now – no need to wait

- being your true and magickal self at all times

Step 4: Call back your energy

The fourth step of the GRACE practice is to call back your energy.

As we discussed in the energetic hygiene section of *Chapter 1.3 – Understanding Energy*, every time you interact with someone, you create an energetic connection with them. Sometimes these connections can be useful, but often they just leave you confused and doubting yourself.

Calling back your energy fills you up again with the energy that actually belongs to you. Much like recognising and appreciating yourself, it helps you to become more full of yourself, enabling you to stay clear and aligned with what's true for you.

This part of the GRACE ritual involves two steps. First, you'll consciously release any energetic connections you've made that don't serve or support you. Then you'll call back your energy from wherever you've 'left' it to 'fill' the newly empty space.

In both cases, you'll use your breath to release and reclaim.

Activity: Calling back your energy

Releasing unwanted energy

Start by visualising the same purple bubble around you that we talked about in *Chapter 1.3 – Understanding Energy*. This will tap you into the Violet Flame of transmutation. Any energy you release will pass through your purple bubble, which cleanses and transforms it before it returns to where it belongs.

Once you've felt into your bubble, release any energy that isn't yours, or that doesn't serve or support you, by exhaling.

On each exhale, set the intention to release whatever no longer serves or supports you.

As you exhale fully, feel your shoulders drop, your jaw relax, your teeth unclench and your eyebrows soften. Feel the energy around you become more spacious.

Know that you're releasing all the energetic connections you've created with people, places or events that don't serve or support you. It doesn't matter whether you created those connections today, this week or years ago. Either way, you're letting them go now.

You may want to breathe out with slightly more force than normal, or just keep your breathing soft. Do what feels right for you in the moment.

Then allow your breath to flow naturally in again.

On your next breath, exhale fully. Again, feel your body relax, release and become lighter.

Continue this for as long as it feels comfortable and good – perhaps just for three breaths or maybe more than ten.

Calling back the energy that's yours

When the releasing feels complete, you'll have made space within yourself that you can call back your own energy into by inhaling. Again, as your energy returns to you, it will pass through your purple bubble, which will cleanse and clear it for your highest good.

First, take a few regular breaths to prepare yourself to call back your energy.

This time, breathe in deeply, right down into your belly.

As you inhale, feel your belly expand.

Set the intention for your energy to return to you, then let your breath flow naturally out again.

As you take your next deep breath in, feel your energy returning to you through time and space. You don't need to know where it was. Just know that as it returns to you, it comes back through your purple bubble, cleansed and clear for your highest good.

Feel yourself being filled up with your own energy and essence. Let yourself feel energised, refreshed and renewed.

After this step...

Once you've finished calling back your energy, take a moment to simply notice how it feels to be quite literally full of yourself.

Notice how your energy feels different from the way it did at the beginning of the practice.

What's changed?

Are you more aware of your energy?

Perhaps you feel more energised, present or content.

Maybe you feel calm and at peace.

Notice any changes, and then move to the next step.

Step 5: Embody

The final step of the GRACE practice is to embody the truth and magick of who you are.

Once you've called back your energy, it's time to take a moment to remember and really savour the truth of who you are.

I like to think of this as 'coming back to your senses'. When you connect with your senses, you can't *not* be in your body. You're quite literally embodied. But beyond that, 'coming back to your senses' connects you to your own consciousness and magick.

Connecting with this truth acts as a barrier to being unduly influenced by everyone around you. This is especially important if you've become selfless and forgotten who you are over time, the way we talked about in *Chapter 2.2 – Getting Full of Yourself.* That's because this connection creates time that you can just spend coming back into a loving, caring relationship with yourself.

This is your time to feel into the truth of who you are again, and enjoy the Magick of You.

Go back to the questions you asked yourself in *Chapter 2.2 – Getting Full of Yourself.* Then spend a little time really feeling into all of the things that are important to you.

Fill yourself up with the energy of your values and desired feelings, and with the answers to those fun questions too. For example, if the animal you chose was a lion, or the flower was a sunflower, feel into what it would be like to actually *be* a lion or a sunflower.

Whatever the energy is, feel it filling you from the tips of your toes to the top of your head, down your arms and out your fingers.

Finally, finish the practice by locking in this energy with a power pose as we talked about in *Chapter 4.6 – The Sacred Pause.*

Spend two minutes (or however long feels right) physically taking up space in your pose, as you allow yourself to take up energetic space with the truth of who you are.

Smile to bring in the energy of expansion

Give yourself permission to be full of your own unique essence.

Then feel your energy filling up your body and spreading through your entire energy system.

Give yourself a moment to enjoy just being you.

Other ways to embody the Magick of You

Other techniques to embody your truth can include:

- asking for what you want, instead of prioritising other people's wants

- asking for something, even if you're not sure you want it, just because you can choose to ask for it

- spending time alone with yourself

- prioritising your own values

- making time for your hobbies and interests, or trying various activities to find out what you like

- trusting your energy and saying no to what doesn't feel right, and yes to what does (even if you're scared of the yes!)

- journaling about topics that are important to you

- thinking back to what you wanted to be as a child – for example, if you wanted to be an astronaut, maybe you value a sense of adventure

- following your curiosity, and doing more of whatever you find interesting, without judging or needing to achieve anything with it

Again, if you'd like to follow along with the practice in 'real-time', visit www.RebeccaAnuwen.com/MagickalBonuses to access videos of the practice.

Key insights to take with you

- The GRACE practice starts with grounding yourself in the present moment, rather than leaving your energy scattered between the past and future.

- It continues by recognising all that you've done (or consciously not done) and appreciating all that you are, to help you start to become full of yourself.

- Finally, it concludes by calling back your energy and embodying your truth and magick, filling you up with energy that serves you.

- This can help you to become more confident in yourself, and bring you a sense of peace and closure, allowing you to fully connect with the Magick of You.

A question to think about

How can you best tailor each step of the GRACE ritual to work perfectly for you?

5.3 | The SACRED Practice

Overview – the SACRED-ness of you

Once you've let go of everything that's not yours, reconnected with everything that is and become full of yourself again, it's so much easier to see what it is that you want and need. When you can see that, it's easier to align yourself with it and start to move towards it... and use the Magick of You to move it towards you.

When you start from this place, you know which actions you need to take to bring what you want to create into being. And, perhaps just as importantly, you know when you need to have patience, let go and let your 'something bigger' play its part in the process.

I created the SACRED practice years ago as a way to align with, and draw on, my own magick. It's a combination of various single practices that I routinely used to connect with and then direct my energy. Over time, I refined these practices into the step-by-step ritual you'll discover in this chapter.

Of course, SACRED is another of the acronyms I love to work with, which – as usual – means the ritual is made up of the first letters of each step:

- **STRIP** off all of your jewellery and crystals, so you can feel YOU.

- **ALIGN** your energy with the truth, priorities and outcomes you identified during the GRACE ritual.

- **CONNECT** with your Higher Self, your inner-most knowing, to receive any messages it might have for you (and help you trust anything you receive).
- **ROOT** into your true essence, so that you're grounded and present.
- **ENCIRCLE** yourself with your energetic shield, supporting your boundaries to keep out whatever isn't yours and protect whatever is.
- **DIRECT** your energy to whatever you want to experience during the coming day, week or month, and then draw it to you with powerful, aligned intentions.

Again, I'll take you through each step in the practice. But, as always, I want you to think of what I'm showing you as a starting point. It's a base template for you to take and make your own. Add anything that feels like it might create a better ritual for you, and change or ignore anything that doesn't resonate.

Give your intuition and creativity free rein, and then enjoy the magick you create.

The best time to practise becoming SACRED

As with the GRACE practice, the best time to do your SACRED ritual is the one that works best and feels most natural and aligned for you.

You could do it straight after you've finished your GRACE practice as a natural follow-on from it.

Or, if you do the GRACE practice each morning or evening, you could do the SACRED practice at the opposite end of the day to reconnect with your magick then.

Or perhaps, if you do the GRACE practice each new moon, you could do the SACRED practice on the full moon.

Another option is to go back to the rhythms and cycles we talked about in *Chapter 4.4 – How to Set Magickal Habits that Work for You.*

Just pick a rhythm that feels right, try it, and then change it up if you find it doesn't work the way you hoped it might.

What to expect once you've finished

There seem to be two extreme schools of thought when it comes to connecting with your magick to create the change you want in your life.

One is that, since everything is spiritual, all you have to do is change your mindset, and maybe say a few magick affirmations, and The Universe will simply fall into line.

The other is that action is the only thing that matters. In this school, taking any action, no matter what it is, will somehow get things moving and naturally bring you closer to your desires.

We've already talked about the fact that doing nothing more than changing your mindset is very rarely enough. You can repeat affirmations to yourself a hundred times a day, but if that's all you're willing to do, nothing's truly likely to change.

But, as we've mentioned a few times in the book now, just taking action for its own sake isn't likely to get you where you want to go either.

The SACRED practice helps to bridge that gap between pure mindset on one hand, and pure action on the other. By the time you've finished the ritual, you should feel:

- a deeper connection with the desires, outcomes and priorities you identified in the GRACE practice (or that you've identified elsewhere)
- a clear alignment with your own truth and the universal wisdom that helps you to easily see the 'right' practical actions that will draw those outcomes towards you
- a sense of confidence and certainty in your ability to take those actions without worrying about what other people think
- a sense of calmness and courage around letting go of the things that no longer serve you in the physical world

Again, it's totally fine if you don't feel all of these things every time you do the SACRED ritual. As with the GRACE practice, just keep tracking, recording and adjusting if you need to until you identify a way that works for you.

Step 1: Strip

We often wear crystals and jewellery (as well as clothes and other accessories) to generate certain feelings, or to energise or recharge us.

In other words, we wear them to change and influence our energy.

That isn't helpful during the SACRED practice, because the ritual is about understanding and connecting with your own energy. Instead, you want to explore how your natural, unassisted energy feels and flows.

Once you're clear on that, you can quickly identify when external energy is influencing you and confidently say, "Actually, that's not mine."

Once you've identified an external influence, you can ground back into your own wisdom. You can re-align with your own values and Higher Self, rather than reacting from fear, judgement or not wanting to let other people down.

So, just for this practice, take anything that changes your energy – including jewellery and crystals – off. You can put them all straight back on afterwards.

Once you've removed everything, get ready to feel into your natural energy.

Activity: Stripping and feeling into your own energy

After taking off your crystals and jewellery, take a moment to feel into your body.

What do you feel?

What sensations do you notice?

Next, feel into the quality of energy within your body.

Is it light and flowing freely, or does it feel tired and sluggish?

Sometimes, it may feel heavy. Sometimes, it'll feel great. And some days, it'll feel somewhere in between.

Finally, feel into the energy field around your physical body, extending out about an arm's width.

Stretch your arms horizontally out to the side to get an idea of how big your energy field is.

Can you feel the edges of the field the way we talked about in the energy-sensing activity in *Chapter 1.3 – Understanding Energy*? Do they crisply, clearly define your space? Or are they a bit wobbly? Perhaps you can't feel anything at all.

Be kind to yourself

Be gentle with yourself as you begin this practice.

Notice what you notice. Don't get distracted by emotions, feelings or judgements about it. Just be a curious observer.

If you find yourself wanting to label things as 'good' or 'bad', try replacing those thoughts with, "Oh, that's interesting!" or, "Hmm, I hadn't noticed that before."

Approach this step with an open heart. Aim to be expansive, playful and curious. Imagine you're going on a fun adventure to learn more about someone you really love and want to support through life. Because that's exactly what you're doing, and that person is *you*.

Remember that there's no right or wrong way to feel. You're just observing, witnessing and collecting data.

It's all just valuable information.

And if you struggle to feel into your own energy, try the energy-sensing activity I mentioned above.

Step 2: Align

Aligning means bringing your energy back into harmony with your core essence and the Magick of You. This frees you from any of the energetic debris that you've accumulated from external sources.

Aligning is all about new beginnings – fresh starts, confidence, optimism, hope and trusting yourself deeply. It's about bringing yourself back into alignment with who you are, with your truth and with your own centre.

Taking the time to regularly come back into alignment with yourself and the Magick of You helps you to clear away anything that you identified in the previous step as 'not yours'.

I like to see this as a way to create breathing space for yourself by pushing away everything that *isn't* you. So instead of anxiety, confusion or overwhelm, you'll experience a moment of calm where you feel centred and grounded.

This is a space where you can collect your thoughts, feel what's really true for you and re-align with what's important to you.

Tools to help you re-align

There are so many tools to help you create that energy alignment. You don't necessarily need any of them, though. You can just follow the process in the 'Align your energy' activity that follows this section.

But for days when you'd like to use a sensory tool, I've included some of my favourites in the list below. Find a simple, quick method that works for you. Use whatever feels right at the time. On different days, you may want to use different techniques.

I'd recommend trying as many as you can, because each technique will change your energy in a different way.

You might find that one technique works best for you when you feel tired and sluggish. Another might be more beneficial when you're overwhelmed, and a different one altogether might work when you feel joyful.

Experiment with the ideas below and find what works best for you at different times. Then simply do whatever most helps you to feel aligned and centred on a given day.

- **Align using smell**: I love working with scents because they create a deep body connection for me. Try carefully burning a herb or incense and wafting the smoke through your energy field. Or try an essential oil you love. Either diffuse it or add a few drops to a carrier oil, rub it on your hands and move them through your energy field.
- **Align using sound**: sound is a powerful tool because it gives you clear, immediate feedback. Consider clapping, using cymbals or other instruments, drumming, clicking your fingers or using your voice to sing or chant. Whatever sound you make, pay attention to its quality as you move or direct it around different parts of your energy field. If you find areas where the sound becomes dull, stuck or 'dirty', keep using your tool there until the sound resonates more clearly.

- **Align using crystals**: my personal favourite is selenite, but you might find other crystals that work better for you. I have a selenite log that feels like a lightsaber when I use it, and another polished oval piece that I run through my energy field like a bar of soap. Other options might include black tourmaline, carnelian, citrine or some form of quartz – either clear, smoky or rose.
- **Align using movement**: sometimes, simply moving your body can help to re-align you. Try dancing, shimmying and shaking, stomping your feet or flicking your hands and feet as though you're flicking the unwanted energy away. You can also rub or massage your skin if that feels better.
- **Align using your breath**: focus on your breath, then breathe in deeply for a count of six and exhale fully for another count of six.
- **Align using water:** as we've mentioned before, you could also make the practice of aligning a part of your bathroom routine. At the end of your shower or bath, spend a few moments visualising the water washing away the energy that isn't yours down the plughole and into the drain.

All of that said, coming back into alignment might just be as simple as taking a deep breath. It might be sitting down with your feet flat on the floor, walking in nature or looking at the sky.

But whatever you choose, you'll need to do it over and over again until the repetition creates an immediate alignment response within you. Eventually, every time you use the technique, your body will say "Oh. Right. This is when we come back into alignment."

I start the alignment process by clearing unwanted energy from above my head to free up the connection with my Higher Self. This ensures that I can connect with my deepest knowing and inner-most wisdom.

Then I move down to my throat to remove anything that's preventing me from speaking or expressing my truth.

Next, I move to the area around my ears to help me clearly hear my intuition.

After that, I clear the area over my shoulders to release any responsibilities I've picked up that aren't mine to carry.

Then, it's down my arms and around my hands. I clear my dominant hand first, so I can let go of what no longer serves or supports me, then my non-dominant hand to receive what I want and need.

Next, I move down the midline of my body. As I do, I notice any part of me that calls for my attention through a twinge or a thought to move it.

After that, I move to the area around my hips and energetic womb space. This is the abdominal area in which some people have a physical womb, but that's not necessary. You might also know this area as the Sacral Chakra or Hara. Regardless of its name, it's an energetic place of darkness, nourishment and creation.

Here, I clear away anything that prevents me from accessing my ability to create, whether I want to create art, words or a loving home.

Then, it's down around my legs, so I can confidently walk forward on my path.

And finally, I focus on the area under my feet to help me take a stand for what's important to me.

Try using this sequence as a starting place, but as with everything else in this book, feel free to change it however you like to suit you.

Lastly, before you finish with this step, take a moment to notice how your energy feels right now. Is it different compared with how it was at the beginning of the Align step?

If so, what's changed? Are you more aware of your energy? Are you starting to notice your energetic edges more clearly?

Or again, perhaps you haven't noticed anything at all.

Again, there's no right answer. Just remain curious and open as you move on to the next step.

Step 3: Connect

The world can sometimes feel overwhelming. Many of my clients say that since they've stepped out onto their own paths in life, they sometimes feel alone. They feel like the people around them don't understand their choices, or that they now experience the world in a very different way from their friends and family.

We talked about the importance of connecting with your 'something bigger' back in *Chapter 3.4 – The Nourished MIND Mindset*. This part of the practice reminds you again that you're not alone. You're part of something much bigger, regardless of your personal beliefs.

When you take a moment to step back and acknowledge that you're part of something greater, your perspective changes.

Think about it. We really are incredibly small. We're each just a tiny little speck of dust on an amazing planet, spinning within its own solar system. And that solar system, in turn, moves within its own galaxy, which is again within its own universe.

I don't say this to take away from the real issues we face as people, communities or societies. I say it because taking a moment to step back and feel the spaciousness around you gives you the ability to breathe. It lets you know that, no matter how you feel in *this* moment, there's more than enough room for you and your biggest feelings and emotions.

It also reassures you that you're allowed to take up space. It helps you to realise that you don't have to keep everything inside. You don't have to do everything alone.

When you connect to your 'something bigger', you begin to remember your connection to your highest knowing and your deepest wisdom. You tap into universal intelligence, and discover that you know so much more, and have access to so many more resources, than you thought you did.

And it only takes a couple of moments to feel that thread of connection.

To connect to universal intelligence and your own deep, intuitive knowing, first close your eyes and put your hand over your heart space.

Visualise a beautiful silver energy filling up your heart space and the whole of your chest.

Let the silver energy nourish, restore and revitalise you.

Once your heart space is full, take some of that silver energy and send it up to the heavens in a silver thread – perhaps to Father Sky, your soul star or your soul family.

It doesn't matter what you believe in. What matters is that you're sending this energy up to connect with your personal 'something bigger' the way we talked about in *Chapter 3.4 – The Nourished MIND Mindset.*

When I do this part of the practice, I like to think of the silver thread as being like the string of a musical instrument. I want my thread to be lovely and taut, just like an instrument string – not slack and wobbly, or out of tune.

That way, any notes, messages, guidance or communications that pass along it flow freely and easily, and are clear and resonant.

Spend some time feeling this connection. If you have a question about your life or just your next step, this is the moment to send the question up your silver thread so your highest wisdom can send the answer back down for you to receive.

Your answer might come immediately, or it might come later as a flash of inspiration over the next few days.

Either way, you'll get the answer you need to hear.

Step 4: Root

Grounding doesn't always sound very sexy or exciting. Let's face it – floating off to other realms to get inspiration and intuition in Step 3: Connect seems like *much* more fun.

But we need to ground ourselves to manifest all the inspiration, dreams and ideas we receive within the physical world. Being grounded and rooted allows you to show up in the world with presence, power, certainty and clarity.

In fact, being grounded is the only way to begin consciously creating the life, communities and world that you want. Yes, you'll get ideas and inspiration for your goals and desires when you're connected to your Higher Self. But the real magick can only happen when you bring that energy back down and root it into the Earth.

That's why bringing the energy of your imagination, dreams and inspiration into reality requires you to root that energy (and yourself). Only then can the things you want manifest in a way you can physically experience. Only then can they become tangible in this world so you can actually have them.

And the only way to make *that* happen is by grounding yourself here on Earth.

Think about a tree

Many trees, especially trees like oaks, grow phenomenally high. When you look at them, you don't see their root system, which is often twice as big as their canopy. After all, the bigger and stronger a root system, the more it can hold above the ground. If a tree with an enormous canopy just has tiny little roots, one strong breeze could bring it crashing down.

Rooting creates strong foundations for the tree. That way, when storms and winds come or people climb it, it can remain standing strong and tall in its space. It can continue to grow and support everything that it looks after – its fruits and acorns, its squirrels and badgers and foxes, and everything else in its ecosystem.

You can't generally see a tree's roots, but they're just as important as everything you see above the ground. They may even be more important.

And it's the same for you. You *also* need deep roots to be able to support yourself, your own ecosystem, and all of the different things that are important to you. You need strong, sturdy roots to stay grounded when you weather your own storms.

Rooting yourself and your energy gives you a solid grounding and a strong foundation. Just like the tree, the deeper you sink your roots, the stronger and more secure you'll be. Then you'll be able to reach further and create more.

When you send your roots down, know that you're rooting into your own wisdom. You're rooting into your strength, your magick and the power of the Earth.

In much the same way as you reached upward to Father Sky in the Connect step, you now sink your roots down to allow Mother Earth to hold you. Know that you can relax completely into this energy of being held, supported and nourished.

Know that you're safe.

And remember that your roots need to be bigger and stronger than everything else you do.

Activity: Rooting into the Earth

To root yourself and your energy, close your eyes and place your hands over your energetic womb space (again: no physical womb necessary).

Imagine this space, and your entire pelvic girdle, filling with a beautiful golden energy.

Let the energy flow around this sacred area, gently releasing anything within you that no longer serves or supports you. Feel it activating whatever needs to be activated.

Then, when you feel good, send some of this golden energy down into the Earth, just like tree roots.

Feel these roots going down into the centre of the Earth, then spreading out to the side to make you feel really safe, stable and held.

Imagine them travelling downward through an underground stream.

Let the cool, refreshing mineral water of this stream wash away any patterns or behaviours that aren't yours, that you've outgrown or that no longer serve or support you.

When you start to feel lighter and cleansed, let this energy travel up through the rest of your energy system, so that your whole body experiences the refreshment.

Next, allow your roots to travel even deeper towards the centre of the Earth, this time passing through crystal caverns.

Notice what crystals are there to support you. You might know each crystal's name, or you may just see a colour, or experience a feeling.

Regardless, let yourself receive nourishment from these crystal allies, feeling their energy travelling up your roots and into the rest of your system.

Once you feel ready, send your golden roots down even further until they reach a beautiful golden ball of energy right in the centre of the Earth.

Allow them to wrap around this ball of energy and become one with it.

Know that the Earth is holding you. Know that you're safe, protected and nourished.

Spend some time really allowing yourself to experience this energy. Again, nothing is expected of you here. You have nothing to do and there's nothing to prove.

Just surrender into the energy of being safe and held.

Finally, when you're ready, come back to your physical body.

Know that you can access this energy of grounded centredness anytime throughout the day.

No matter what comes your way or how buffeted by life's experiences you may feel, you can always reconnect with your roots to feel grounded and anchored once more.

And again, before you move to the next step, check in and see how your energy feels different compared with the beginning of the practice.

What's changed?

Are you more aware of your energy?

Perhaps you're starting to notice how you feel within your own body.

Maybe you feel more present and grounded.

Regardless, notice any changes.

Note that you can also use this activity as a way to ground yourself in the GRACE practice too.

Step 5: Encircle

When your boundaries are strong, clear and backed with the power of your presence, other people can recognise and honour them.

Back in *Chapter 1.3 – Understanding Energy*, we talked about using a purple bubble to create clear boundaries between your energy and everyone else's. In this step, you're going to create that bubble and clearly see (or otherwise sense) it surrounding you.

This powerful practice helps you to feel safe and establish strong, tangible boundaries. That's essential, because as your energetic boundaries become stronger, your personal boundaries in life strengthen too. You start making those boundaries a priority, and you quickly notice when something or someone compromises them.

You get clearer on what you will and won't accept, and you get more confident about speaking up when you need to.

Perhaps you feel more comfortable telling someone that their behaviour around you isn't OK. Maybe you confidently say no to something that you don't want to do. Or you might start setting limits around your resources, both with yourself and other people.

Plus, when life gets too busy and everything feels like it's 'too close' and overwhelming, it's hard to think clearly. Encircling your energy creates space around you, making it easier to step back slightly from everything. This gives you the sense of being able to breathe more easily and get a clearer perspective on the overwhelm.

That space then allows you to say, "Oh! That thought, that belief, that doubt in myself – that's not mine! That's actually somebody else's!" Maybe it's your mum being overprotective. Perhaps it's your culture expecting you to follow this career path. Or perhaps it's society telling you that you have to follow this route in life to be successful...

Regardless, that space helps you to clearly identify which thoughts and feelings are yours, and which you're absorbing or are being projected onto you. And that clarity makes it easier to know what you need to do next. If whatever comes up is yours, you can address it. If not, you can remind yourself that it doesn't belong to you, and set it down again.

Depending on the day and what feels right, you might try different colours and textures for your bubble. But always start with the basic purple to connect with the Violet Flame.

Activity: **Encircling your energy with a purple bubble**

Imagine yourself surrounded by that beautiful, shiny, purple bubble

Imagine your bubble being light and moveable, just like a real bubble.

Feel yourself safe and centred within it.

Remember that your energy system typically extends out to an arm's width away from your body, and start feeling your purple bubble around its edges.

Notice how your energy feels with the bubble around it.

Next, try changing the size of your bubble.

First, in your mind's eye, imagine pulling your purple bubble in closer to you.

How does that feel? Is it better or more restrictive?

Next, imagine pushing your purple bubble out much wider, as far as you can imagine.

How does that feel? Does it feel expansive or overly vulnerable?

Play around with your bubble, until it feels great to you.

Lastly, try customising your bubble

If it feels right to, imagine changing the texture of the bubble around you and see how it feels.

Or alternatively, imagine adding a layer of paint, in any thickness you want, being sure to cover all areas of your bubble.

Take a moment to really savour your own energy within this clearly defined space that you've created.

As you practise visualising your purple bubble more, you'll start to notice when other people's energy tries to enter your space and unduly influence you over the day.

When this happens, you'll be ready and prepared to respond to it, rather than reacting.

You'll also feel calmer because you're responding from a place of presence and clarity, rather than feeling overwhelmed by the events and people around you.

Step 6: Direct

When you reach this stage of the SACRED practice, you're in the perfect place to manifest exactly what you desire.

Your energy is flowing clearly, you're connected to your Higher Self and you're rooted into your truth. In this moment, you're not influenced by anyone else's judgements, expectations or desires.

You're ready to direct your energy wherever you want it, into whichever practice, or actions you choose.

You might decide to do something really tangible. Maybe there's a task on your to-do list you want to finish, or a conversation that you know you need to have.

You could also direct your energy into experiencing more of your values and desired feelings, and bring those front and centre in your life.

Regardless, choose an intention, then feel into the core feelings, values or experiences that go with accomplishing that intention. Imagine what you'll feel like once you've had that difficult conversation, or ticked that item off your to-do list.

Imagine and feel into these things as if they've already happened. Your body and mind don't understand the difference between reality and imagination. So just feel your intention as if it had already happened.

As you do this, you're saying to The Universe, "Thank you. More of this, please."

You can feel or picture the outcome you choose in any way you want.

Maybe you'll 'see' your desire as a colour around you. Perhaps it's a crystal or a flower, or a sign over your chest. The details don't matter. There's no right or wrong way to do this, as long as you're connecting with and feeling into the experience.

Your energy is running free, clear and uninterrupted by the noise and busyness of life. So what do you actually want now, and what do you need to do to create it?

Close your eyes, put your hands on your body, and ask what the best use of your time and energy is.

Will you focus on an activity, or on experiencing more of your values?

Maybe you want to start – or stop – doing something.

Perhaps you need to reach out to someone for support.

This isn't about trying to do everything. It's about deciding how you're going to direct your newly aligned energy.

Then, once you've decided, spend a few moments really feeling into the energy of your choice, as if it had already happened.

Finally, when you're ready, set a timer for two minutes (or however long feels right for you). Then move into a power pose as we discussed in *Chapter 4.6 – The Sacred Pause.*

When your timer goes off, you've completed the SACRED practice.

Let yourself smile, and move about your day feeling centred, grounded and aligned with what you want to create.

Again, if you'd like to follow along with the practice in real time, visit www.RebeccaAnuwen.com/MagickalBonuses to access videos of the practice.

Key insights to take with you

- The SACRED ritual is about taking the newfound clarity you developed in the GRACE practice, reconnecting with your priorities and desires, and then moving towards them.

- To do this, you first strip off anything external that influences your energy to feel into your own truth, then align with it.

- Next, you connect with your own intuitive knowing and universal intelligence, and root deep into the Earth to strengthen and stabilise yourself

- Finally, you encircle your energy field with a bubble to keep your own energy in and other influences out, before directing your energy into your chosen action to create magick.

A question to think about

How can you best tailor each step of the SACRED ritual to work perfectly for you?

Conclusion

Next steps

How do you feel about everything you've learnt?

You've done it – you've reached the end of *Magickal Knickers and other ways to create a life of intention.* Congratulations!

Take a deep breath and let it out slowly. Let yourself recognise the magnitude of the journey you've just been on. If I've done the job I wanted to do when I set out to write this book, you'll now have dozens, maybe even hundreds, of ideas you want to try out.

And while a flood of ideas can be wonderful, it can also be incredibly overwhelming and leave you with no clue about where to start. So before you do anything else, let's briefly recap the path you've walked to get here from the beginning of this book.

- **In Section 1: Key Concepts**, you learnt about some of the core background concepts that underlie everything else you explored in the rest of the book. You discovered what exactly your magick is, how it can help you to create the life you want, and how intuition and energy play a role in the process.

- **In Section 2: Your Magickal Life Philosophy**, you discovered how your life philosophy can help or hinder your ability to manifest your desires. You also explored what you need to do to develop a philosophy that supports you in reclaiming your magick.

- **In Section 3: Your Magickal Mindset**, you learnt about the importance of maintaining a supportive mindset, and what that does and doesn't mean. I also introduced you to a range of techniques to help you keep your mindset motivated, intentional, nourished and dedicated.

- **In Section 4: Magickal Habits**, you explored how to start doing the work and taking the action that will bring your desires into being. You learnt how to take ordinary, everyday habits and make them magickal, and how doing so could support you in taking the bigger actions that directly move you forward with your dreams.

- **In Section 5: Magickal Practices**, you explored the differences between habits, practices and rituals, and how each can play a part in creating the outcomes you want in your life. I also shared a couple of my favourite rituals with you and offered ideas to help you tailor them to your unique goals and life circumstances.

That's a lot of information to take in. So if you need to step back, grab a cup of tea and just let yourself process it all for a few breaths, I totally understand.

Where will you start your unique journey?

I know I've said it several times over the course of the book, but it bears repeating: the rituals and habits we talk about are called 'practices' because you have to *practise* them. And the more you practise them, the more effective they become.

So while, of course, a supportive philosophy and mindset are important, they're mostly important because they set you up to take action. They don't miraculously do the work for you – instead they make it easier for you to do it for yourself. They reduce the inertia that can keep you stuck and unable to move forward. They can also help to create the belief in yourself and your power that reassures you that the action you take actually *matters*.

All of which means that now is the perfect time to decide exactly where you're going to start putting what you've learnt into practice.

I said in the Introduction that, on their second time around, many people will want to go right back to the beginning and work their way through the book section by section. If that sounds like the perfect path for you, great. I invite you to flick back to the beginning of Section 2 *right now* and start reading and completing the activities to create your Magickal Life Philosophy.

Or, if that's not practical at the moment, get out your planner or bring up the calendar on your phone. Make a clear decision about when you WILL come back to it, and schedule it in before you shut this book again.

If you're comfortable with your life philosophy as it is now, but know your day-to-day mindset could do with some help, feel free to start with Section 3 instead. Again though, either flip back and start re-reading that section right now, or make a firm date with yourself to do it later.

And the same is true if you want to start with habits, or with creating rituals for yourself.

There's no one right place to begin. But wherever you start, the key is to either take action now, or schedule it in for a specific time later. What you don't want to let yourself do is shut the book with the best of intentions to pick it up again... and then forget about reclaiming your magick completely because life gets in the way.

So once you've taken that mindful breath, celebrated the journey up till now and finished that cup of tea, decide where you want to start practising what you've learnt.

And then simply... start.

You don't have to take this journey alone

I know I made the process of starting to reclaim the Magick of You sound incredibly simple in the previous sentence. And in some ways, it really is just that easy. But in others – let's be realistic – there's a *lot* that can get in your way.

If you've always prioritised everyone else's opinions, thoughts, judgements and values, it can feel almost impossible to put your foot down and prioritise yourself, especially at first.

Even if the people around you don't get upset at you or tell you you're selfish or inconsiderate, your own inner critic will no doubt have a field day. You'll second-guess yourself over and over again. You'll find yourself acting in ways you've promised you wouldn't anymore, simply because they're so ingrained.

When this happens, it's important to recognise that it's all part of the process. Breaking long-term patterns takes time and repeated effort. You probably won't completely let go of habits that have taken you 20 or 30 years to form in a matter of weeks, or even months.

That's OK. There's an (allegedly) ancient Japanese saying: fall down seven times, stand up eight. It doesn't matter how many times you've fallen down, as long as you make the decision to get back up after the most recent one.

The good news is that you don't have to do any of this alone. If you want to connect with other like-minded people who are each on a journey to reclaim their own magick, I have a FREE online community that you're welcome to explore.

Find out more about us – and learn how to join – at www. RebeccaAnuwen.com/magickal-community/.

Or, if you're more of a solitary traveller, you'll find videos and other resources to support your journey through this book at www.RebeccaAnuwen.com/MagickalBonuses.

And for general content that reminds you of just how powerful and magickal you are, plus tips on how to live a more magickal life, you can also follow me through:

- **Instagram**: I'm @themodernwitchway there

- **my newsletter**: go to my website at www.RebeccaAnuwen.com and sign up

A final parting thought...

If there's one core message I want you to take from *Magickal Knickers and other ways to create a life of intention*, it's that no one – including me – can tell you how your journey should look.

No one can tell you what your goals and dreams should or shouldn't be.

No one can tell you which techniques will help you to bring them into being the fastest, or the most powerfully, or the most effectively.

The only person who knows what's right for you is you. You might not realise you know it, but I promise that if you get still enough and create enough space around you, you'll start to become aware of the right way forward for you.

Perhaps you'll get a sense of the overall direction you feel called to head in – what many people call your 'life purpose'. Or perhaps you'll just get a feel for your immediate next step.

Either way, trust yourself and listen to your inner knowing. Remember: if you later decide that following this path is no longer right for you, that's OK. You can always change your mind and choose again at any time. And you'll probably be richer for the experience of having at least tried it.

Whatever you do though, don't keep putting off prioritising yourself, your goals and your dreams until that mythical 'someday when'. You only get one wild and precious life, as Mary Oliver described it.

You're already a significant part of the way through your 4,000 weeks. Don't let the weeks you still have left slip away while you 'just take care of' this priority for someone else and then the next and then the next after that.

Play with the techniques in this book. Change them up to suit you. Develop completely new ones if you want to. Explore and experiment.

Through it all, walk your own path.

It's the only way to truly reclaim and embody the Magick of You.

With love and magick

Rebecca
xx

Acknowledgements

Thank you! Thank you! And thank you some more!

Tanja, thank you for taking my ideas and words and making them into something far more comprehensible than what I gave you. Thank you for allowing me (and the book) the time and space to evolve through a constant stream of new ideas. I know that you expect that from me now, haha, but thank you anyway.

And thank you for your dedication to making my words accessible with the thoughtful 'I know it's implied, but let's make it obvious' stance you take with my ideas and concepts.

If you were a pair of knickers, you'd be the favourite pair that someone always feels most like themselves in.

Janice, I'm incredibly grateful for the possibly hundreds of (and, let's be honest, hundreds more) text messages and the copious amounts of tea we've shared. You've consistently encouraged me and sometimes given me a much-needed New York nudge in the right direction to help bring this book to life.

Even though we live very different lives, there's so much shared magick between us.

If you were a pair of knickers, you'd be bright, bold and very eye-catching.

Grant, thank you for all of your creativity, design skills and incredible attention to detail. And thanks also for always exploring all of my ideas, even the terrible ones, with as much enthusiasm as me.

If you were a pair of knickers, you'd have a complex geometric pattern and be very easy to wear.

Finally, members of the Witch Academy and Magickal Community, thank you for saying yes to your magick and consistently embracing more of it each day. The world is a brighter, more joyful and magickal place because of each and every one of you.

If you were a pair of knickers... well, you'd be the best pair in the world!

About Rebecca

Rebecca is on a mission to create a world where people feel supported and confident to pursue their wildest dreams and desires...

... one where they can uncover their truth, power and magick with simple everyday choices

... where they can tackle even the deep work with awe, wonder and fun (whilst of course wearing their #magickalknickers!)

More than 20 years ago, Rebecca trained in kinesiology. Her booked-out practice taught her that whenever people were suffering, the root cause was almost always emotional.

Then, over the years, her work evolved to include people who didn't feel like they needed conventional healing. Instead, they wanted to be more authentically themselves: more confident, self-expressive and unapologetic.

And today, she helps those who want to get back in touch with the inner voice they've silenced and repressed for so long.

Rebecca's experience and training make her the perfect guide to help you break free of judgements and expectations to reclaim your magick (and upgrade the contents of your knicker drawer).

So grab your knickers – it's go time!

Appendices

Appendix A: Quick-reference Activity Guide

This is a quick-reference guide to the activities and exercises you've done in your journey through the book. It will allow you to flip straight to a particular activity if you decide you'd like to do it again at some later time.

Chapter	Activity name	Activity summary
1.1	Noticing the magick that's already present	See your RAS in action by setting an intention to see something during the day, and noticing the different ways in which it then shows up for you.
1.2	Identifying your intuition when it speaks	Note the different ways in which your intuition speaks to you, and then record how intuitive nudges show up and the results of either following or ignoring them.
1.3	Getting a sense of your own energy	Explore the boundaries of your energy field, play with an energy ball, and then see how it responds to your intentions for it.

Chapter	Activity name	Activity summary
2.1	Feeling into a philosophy that supports you	Identify the values or feelings you want to ground your life philosophy in, and then consciously feel what it would be like to experience them in your everyday life.
2.1	Creating your Magickal Life Philosophy	Use the feelings and experiences you want more of in your life to create a supportive life philosophy that helps you to reclaim your magick.
2.2	Questions to help you fill yourself up with your truth	Answer two serious questions (or a collection of fun ones) that help you to gain clearer insight into what's really important to you.
2.3	What's in a name?	Think about how you want to describe yourself, and explore the power of the tiny word 'yet'.

Chapter	Activity name	Activity summary
2.4	Reviewing your knickers	Look at each pair of underwear you own in turn to see how it aligns with and reflects your Magickal Life Philosophy.
2.4	Living your Magickal Life Philosophy	Choose three to five daily morning activities and experiment with bringing more of your Magickal Life Philosophy into each.
3.1	Exploring your history with manifesting and mindset	Identify a situation where you successfully achieved a desire, and another where you didn't, and compare the two.
3.2	Your motivational why	Dig down into the layers of your motivation for an outcome or intention you want to achieve.
3.2	Regularly checking in with yourself	Ask yourself three essential questions each time you encounter an obstacle to achieving your desire.

Chapter	Activity name	Activity summary
3.3	Examining your boundaries	Look at your boundaries in different areas of your life and honestly evaluate how clearly you communicate them with the people in your life.
3.3	Strengthening your boundaries	Focus on one of the boundaries you know you need to strengthen and create a plan to support you in maintaining it.
3.4	Exploring the 'something bigger' that's right for you	Think back on the relationship, if any, you developed with your 'something bigger' as a child, and decide what relationship you'd like to have with it today.
3.5	Dedicating to the Magick of You	Create a formal-yet-simple ritual to dedicate yourself to your desire and your magick as a whole.
3.6	Letting go of your inner good girl	Use an imaginary credit system to help you track your success in maintaining a boundary over time.

Chapter	Activity name	Activity summary
3.6	Letting go of the negativity guilt	Learn to recognise the truth of your negative thoughts without denying your experience or feelings.
3.6	Letting go of the fear of judgement	Explore your relationship with judgement and identify how to prioritise your desires when it occurs.
3.6	Letting go of good vibes only	Experience the transformational power of sacred anger, rather than trying to stuff the feeling down and pretend it doesn't exist.
3.7	Magickal MIND mindset check-in cheat sheet	Quickly check how you're doing on the four elements of a Magickal MIND mindset.
4.1	Exploring your current habits	Take quick stock of the habits you currently do successfully and examine how they support your Magickal Life Philosophy.

Chapter	Activity name	Activity summary
4.2	Rating the quality of your energetic influences	Investigate how the energetic influences that your current habits create support or undermine you.
4.3	The SCAT pages process	Use the SCAT technique to clear your mind and keep everything 'moving' in your life the way you want it to.
4.3	Doing gratitude your way	Use gratitude or appreciation to bring you back to your senses and make the ordinary magickal.
4.3	Practising visualisation	Strengthen your visualisation skills using the senses that work best for you.
4.3	Nature bathing	Allow yourself to switch off the pressures of daily life and truly experience being in nature.
4.4	RIFFing an everyday ritual	Identify an existing everyday habit and explore how you could make it more meaningful and intentional.

Chapter	Activity name	Activity summary
4.5	Creating a magickal day	Experiment with the ideas in *Chapter 4.5 – Magickal Mornings and Enchanted Evenings* to find what works for you.
4.6	Taking a Sacred Pause	Try the simplest possible version of the Sacred Pause practice before you think about how you could incorporate it into your day.
5.1	Recording your weekly (or monthly) progress	Make a regular time each week or month to reflect on your magickal practice progress.
5.2	Grounding yourself in the present	Create a 'lightning rod' for the energies of anxiety or overwhelm, and a foundation for the rest of the GRACE practice.
5.2	Recognising yourself	Recognise everything you've done, and everything you've chosen NOT to do, and savour that recognition.

Chapter	Activity name	Activity summary
5.2	Appreciating yourself	Appreciate yourself for not only everything you've done, but everything you are as well.
5.2	Calling back your energy	Fill yourself up with the energy that belongs to you by calling it back from wherever you've left it.
5.2	Embodying the Magick of You	Connect with your senses and feel into the truth of who you are and what's important to you.
5.3	Stripping and feeling into your own energy	Remove everything that changes your energy, feel how your own energy flows, and sense the edges of its field.
5.3	Aligning your energy	Bring your energy back into harmony with your own core essence and free yourself from any energetic debris.
5.3	Connecting to universal intelligence	Connect to your 'something bigger', and through it, your highest knowing and your deepest wisdom.

Chapter	Activity name	Activity summary
5.3	Rooting into the Earth	Imagine golden roots of energy stabilising, supporting and connecting you with the energy of the Earth.
5.3	Encircling your energy with a purple bubble	Use the purple bubble technique to help you differentiate what's yours and what isn't, and give you space to breathe.
5.3	Directing your energy	Decide how you'll use your newly aligned energy by directing your magick towards a specific intention.

Appendix B: Resources I've Referred To

I've mentioned or quoted from a few different resources over the course of the book.

If you'd like to check them out, you can find more information about them below.

Books

- *Four Thousand Weeks*, by Oliver Burkeman
- *Atomic Habits*, by James Clear
- *The Science of Storytelling*, by Will Storr
- *Lost Connections*, by Johann Hari

Articles

Forbes article on writing by hand compared to digitally: https://www.forbes.com/sites/nancyolson/2016/05/15/three-ways-that-writing-with-a-pen-positively-affects-your-brain/

Louise Hay's article on mirror work: https://www.louisehay.com/what-is-mirror-work/

Anything else

Mind's *Nature and mental health* article: https://www.mind.org.uk/information-support/tips-for-everyday-living/nature-and-mental-health/how-nature-benefits-mental-health/

Amy Cuddy's *Body Language May Shape Who You Are* TED talk: https://www.amycuddy.com/media/video

Mary Oliver's *A Summer Day* poem: - https://www.loc.gov/programs/poetry-and-literature/poet-laureate/poet-laureate-projects/poetry-180/all-poems/item/poetry-180-133/the-summer-day/

Printed in Great Britain
by Amazon